ROCKET MAN

BY STEVEN DIETZ

★

★

DRAMATISTS
PLAY SERVICE
INC.

ROCKET MAN
Copyright © 2003, Steven John Dietz

All Rights Reserved

SPECIAL NOTE

SPECIAL NOTE ON SONGS AND RECORDINGS

*This play is dedicated
to the memory of Bob Nadir —
actor, builder, friend.*

AUTHOR'S NOTE

"For if there is a sin against life, it consists perhaps
not so much in despairing of life, as in hoping for
another life — and in eluding the implacable
grandeur of this one."
          —*Albert Camus,* Summer in Algiers

Is there another world? Another life? I ask this not so much in a scientific or spiritual context, but in a personal one. Is there another
world — parallel to our own — in which life has dealt us the same
hand but we chose to play our cards differently? A world in which
the "road not taken" was followed to its end? *Rocket Man* is my
attempt to imagine such a world.

It's been said that the history of human thought is the history of
regrets. We move through life with one eye on the present and one
on the future — and all the while our heart is making an inventory
of missed chances along the way. Regrets are insidious and unre-
lenting. They are also, in their own way, rather comforting. For one,
they require very little of us. They're usually static, frozen safely in
the past ("Well, it's too late to do anything about that now."etc.).
Secondly, they're easy to maintain. We're not expected to cultivate
our regrets like we are our "dreams." We can blissfully ignore them
for years (at times "the unexamined life" is a godsend) and then take
them out on a rainy day and wallow in them with impunity.
Thirdly, they play well in public since we are seldom the only one in
the room nursing a regret (or two). They allow us, in fact, the freedom to construct a remarkable past ("If only I had done that when
I had the chance, everything would be different."), which is infi-
nitely easier than the tangible work of creating a future. Finally, and
most crucially, our regrets almost never call our bluff. We are seldom
given the "second chance" that we claim so desperately to want.
Thank goodness for that. Imagine a world in which we were forced
to go back and "get it right this time" — and then had to live with
the consequences (perhaps) of making an even worse choice than we
did before. The past is a one-way street with good reason.

Which brings us to the present. The present alone is the home to action — that tiny, fleeting window between hope and regret. How then to spend it? What is to be done? In researching this play, I found these words by the remarkable landscape architect Frederick Law Olmsted:

> "Let us help each other then to give our thoughts a
> practical turn. There is great work wants doing in
> this generation, let us off-jacket and go about it."

The answer, like space, is both obvious and infinite: We must combat our regrets (as best we can) with action. We must not rest on conviction, when conduct is required. And (with apologies to Disney) we must disenthrall ourselves with "wishing." Though the virtual world can be surfed, the real world must still be wrestled.

Rocket Man is the story of a man determined to transcend the boundaries of his life, determined to be granted that elusive "second chance." To do so, he must investigate what Camus called "this measureless universe where my adventure takes place." There is no telling what he will find there. For if our regrets are daunting, so too are the consequences of our actions. Knowingly or not, we affect the world with our every breath.

—*Steven Dietz*
28 January '98
Santa Monica, CA

ROCKET MAN received its world premiere by the Arizona Theatre Company (David Ira Goldstein, Artistic Director; Jessica L. Andrews, Managing Director) in Tucson, Arizona, on March 6, 1998. It was directed by David Ira Goldstein; the set design was by Scott Weldin; the costume design by Carolyn Keim; the lighting design by Rick Paulsen; the sound design by Brian Jerome Peterson; and the stage manager was Glenn Bruner. The cast was as follows:

DONNY .... Kurt Rhoads
BUCK .... Michael Winters
TRISHA .... Carol Roscoe
RITA .... Pamela Stewart
LOUISE .... Lauren Tewes

The understudy for DONNY and BUCK was Robert Nadir.

CHARACTERS

DONNY — a man in his early forties
BUCK — his friend, fifties
TRISHA — his daughter, sixteen
RITA — his ex-wife, late thirties
LOUISE — his friend and co-worker, forties

TIME

This present. And another one.

PLACE

The attic of an American home.

Behind you the windows of the town
blink on and off, the houses close down;
ahead the voices fade like music
over deep water, and then are gone;
even the sudden, tumbling finches
have fled into smoke, and the one road
whitened in moonlight leads everywhere.

—*Philip Levine, "Ask for Nothing"*

ROCKET MAN

ACT ONE

Scene 1

*Light shines from underneath the closed attic door – coming
from the hallway outside. Donny, carrying a cardboard box
under his arm, opens the door and steps into the darkened
room. Donny sets the box down and plugs an assemblage of
numerous extension cords and adapters into a single wall outlet at eye level, and — a roomful of discarded lamps comes to
life, revealing — the cluttered attic. Filling the room are the
remnants of a life spent in this house. Donny closes the door
and slides a bolt, locking it. He turns to the audience and
smiles, speaking to them.*

DONNY. Near this house — at Fourth and Grove — there is an
intersection. I encounter it every day. And for twenty years I've
stood at that intersection pushing the little "Crosswalk Signal"
button. And after pushing it, I stand there … and stand there …
and *stand there* … waiting for the light to change. And the longer
I wait, the more I push the button. Over time, I've tried variations.
Pushing in a syncopated rhythm. Pushing it a certain number of
times — seven, thirteen, twenty-nine. Sometimes I thought it was
dependent on time of day, or season, or some complex city-wide
pattern known only to a select few. But through it all, for years
now … I've stood there … trusting in some "invisible traffic signal logic." Until today. Today I brought a crowbar. *(He reaches into*

11

the box he brought into the room, and removes an object, shows it to the audience — It is, indeed, a "Crosswalk Signal Box." It features the universal icon of the walking person; the words "Push Button for Walk Signal"; and, of course, the button.) And after I removed it from the post, I unscrewed the plate in back [front]. And I looked inside. *(He shows the audience the uncovered back [or front] of the Signal Box.) Nothing!* Not a *single* wire. Just a lone button attached to nothing but the finger of a stupid pedestrian filled with hope and trust. I thought you should know this. And, I take great pleasure in what I'm about to say: *(He lifts the Signal Box above his head and exclaims, buoyantly —)* I knew it! All these years — all the times I stood there in the rain, pushing that button till my fingers ached — I KNEW IT! We demand the *illusion* of involvement. Just give us a button! — that's all we ask! — 'cause as long as we have a button to push, we assume we're *making things happen.* But the fact is: *the light changes when it wants to — we have nothing to do with it! (There is loud knocking on the attic door. Donny puts the Signal Box back into the cardboard box.)*
BUCK'S VOICE. Donny! Hey, Donny — you up here? *(Donny turns and goes to the door.)* What the hell is — Donny, hey, c'mon, open up — it's me. *(Donny unlocks and opens the door. Buck steps in, holding a large hand saw. He inadvertently gestures with it as he speaks.)*
DONNY. Morning, Buck.
BUCK. What are you doing?
DONNY. I'm in my attic.
BUCK. With the door locked?
DONNY. Well — yeah — with the door —
BUCK. What are you doing, Donny? Are you cleaning?
DONNY. Well — yeah — sort of —
BUCK. Are you moving?
DONNY. Well — no — I'm just —
BUCK. I have a lot of questions, Donny —
DONNY. I see that —
BUCK. Because I'm on my way to have my hair cut — and I'm runnin' late — so I'm doin' about eighty past your house tryin' to make my eleven-fifteen with Loreen — and just then I see something, Donny. Do you want to explain?

DONNY. What's to explain? (*Donny now begins to move about the attic, sorting through the paraphernalia, boxing it up. From time to time he carries boxes or items out the door and places them in the [unseen] hallway. Note: Donny takes great pleasure in this activity. He is a man putting in motion a plan which he fervently believes in. Buck follows him around the attic, adamantly —*)

BUCK. I've, what, I've known you for, what — twenty years? Thirty? I moved you and Rita into this house. I baby-sat Trisha while you and Rita went to dinner and yelled at each other. I took you to Mexico after the divorce —

DONNY. Yeah, lotta great memories, Buck.

BUCK. "Here's My Life — Make An Offer." (*Pause.*) There's a sign on your front lawn, Donny, and that's what it says: "Here's My Life — Make An Offer." So, do you want to explain? Your house is empty and your life is all over the lawn. People are picking through your stuff like a boneyard.

DONNY. Good for them.

BUCK. Are you going away?

DONNY. Yeah.

BUCK. Where?

DONNY. I don't know, yet.

BUCK. You don't — what? — DONNY! — look at me. You haven't seemed like yourself lately, and even though some people pay good money for that feeling, I'm worried about you. (*Donny stops his work and looks up at Buck.*) Now, please …

DONNY. (*Simply.*) I've been losing days, Buck. Sometimes entire weeks. They just fly past and I don't even see them. I wrote a check at the grocery store and the woman handed it back — I'd written the wrong month.

BUCK. Well, I've done that, too —

DONNY. I wasn't even *close,* Buck. I was three months off. It keeps happening — like time is playing tricks with me.

BUCK. They say it's not as trustworthy as we think — that it loops back on itself. But, that's no reason to —

DONNY. My life is littered with *things,* Buck — and my days are getting lost amid the clutter. So, I want to be rid of it. Rid of it all. You need a saw?

BUCK. Hmm? (*Looking down at the saw in his hand, realizing.*) Oh,

13

well, it was down there and another guy was about to grab it —
DONNY. You need it, it's yours.
BUCK. I want to make you an offer.
DONNY. You don't have to —
BUCK. But, I want to.
DONNY. Please, just —
BUCK. Eight bucks.
DONNY. For *that?*
BUCK. *(Opening his wallet.)* You're my best friend, Donny. I want to do right by you.
DONNY. Fifteen.
BUCK. What?
DONNY. Fifteen.
BUCK. For *this?* Donny, are you —
DONNY. Anybody else I'd ask twenty. For you: fifteen. *(Buck stops, stares at him.)*
BUCK. Ten.
DONNY. Thirteen.
BUCK. Eleven-fifty. *(Donny seems to nod, but says nothing. Buck once again begins to reach into his wallet, as Donny says —)*
DONNY. Twelve. *(Buck stares at Donny, hard — then relents. He hands him the bills from his wallet. Donny takes them and folds them into his palm.)* Good. Now, give me a hand, huh? *(As Buck turns his head to survey the attic, Donny quickly slips the bills into a pocket of Buck's shirt or jacket. Buck is unaware of this. Donny returns to his work.)*
BUCK. Haven't been up here in years. Eaves are in good shape — looks like it seals up real well.
DONNY. It's *airtight* — I made sure of that.
BUCK. *(Looking at the power outlet.)* You want me to put a light switch in here? All these cords aren't a good idea, Donny.
DONNY. I'll take care of it.
BUCK. Weren't you gonna make this attic into your — what-do-you-call-it? — into your —
DONNY. Yeah — that was the plan —
BUCK. You ran electricity, and a gas line, and everything up here —
DONNY. Yeah, and here it sits. The gas line is capped. Skylight's covered over with insulation.

BUCK. This was gonna be your — you know — c'mon, help me out — what's the word — your —

DONNY. *(Sharp.)* Nothing. It never happened. *(Buck stares at Donny, then asks —)*

BUCK. Do you ever hear voices, Donny? *(Donny stops working, looks at Buck.)* When you're up here alone. Do you ever...?

DONNY. No. *(They stare at each other. Then, by some kind of silent consent, they drop the matter completely. Donny returns to work. Buck checks his pocket watch.)*

BUCK. I should call the salon and re-schedule.

DONNY. *(Referring to Buck's lack of hair.)* All due respect, pal: I think your salon days are behind you.

BUCK. What, a guy can't *treat* himself? A guy, what, okay, so I'm growin' a little more forehead every day — I mean who *isn't,* Donny? — but, what, do I have to be *punished* for that?!

DONNY. I'm just saying that you —

BUCK. I see Loreen once a week now, Donny. It is now a *part of my life.*

DONNY. Okay, already —

BUCK. Because you know what, Donny? — you know what happens there?

DONNY. Look, let's —

BUCK. *I get my head touched.* I mean, sure, Loreen makes a few snipping noises to give me the illusion of having, you know, hair. But mainly, Donny, she just *touches my head.* Rubs shampoo on it. Lotion. Presses her stubby, wet fingers into my scalp. And I close my eyes. And she tells me about her husband and family. And I listen and nod. But I'm not hearing a word. I'm just there to be touched. *(Pause.)* Never knew how bad I missed it. Ten years now since Grace passed on. How many days — do the math, Donny — how many days and weeks is that without ever being touched? *By anyone. (Pause.)* Too long. *(He turns to Donny.)* You think I'm nuts?

DONNY. No.

BUCK. Well, stay tuned. I'll use your phone and be right back. *(Buck starts for the attic door —)*

DONNY. The phone was the first thing to go.

BUCK. You gave away your ph —

DONNY. All of it, Buck. Now, give me a hand and I'll touch

15

your head. *(Buck pulls a few envelopes and magazines from his back pocket. Hands them to Donny.)*

BUCK. Oh, I nearly forgot — here's your mail. *(Donny flips through the magazines. Buck begins to carry items out into the hallway.)* What's with those, anyway? *Astronomy. Omni.* All that stars and Martians and godknowswhat? Since when do you —

DONNY. I got interested, Buck —

BUCK. Yeah, right, I mean, sure, but —

DONNY. Something wrong with that?

BUCK. No, it's just, you know, you're a surveyor, Donny — you're a *ground man* — you're a *measure the earth* kind of guy.

DONNY. People acquire interests, Buck —

BUCK. Yeah, right, but I've never known you to —

DONNY. It is now a *part of my life. (Buck stares at him. Then, they keep working.)*

BUCK. How's Trisha?

DONNY. Turns sixteen next week. I've got a surprise party planned for her. I want you there.

BUCK. I'll be there.

DONNY. You're her godfather — don't forget. Should anything happen to me, you become her —

BUCK. Donny — I'll be there. I'll bring chips. *(Beat.)* You *sure* her birthday's next week?

DONNY. Yeah, why?

BUCK. Just wondered.

DONNY. *Sixteen* — how can that be? My daughter is somehow old enough to drive.

BUCK. The more things change the more different they get.

DONNY. *(Accustomed to ignoring Buck's axioms.)* She's become a *young woman,* Buck. I was not told this would happen.

BUCK. Wait till she's out in the world — it only gets weirder. I mean, here I am, my kids are grown — and I barely know 'em anymore. James is doing something called "competitive aerobics" — jumpin' around in nothin' but leotards and a tan. And Susan, of all things, ends up in *law enforcement.*

DONNY. They're doing okay, Buck —

BUCK. I'm talking about *me.* I'm the one that — *(Buck stops, lifts something out from amid the clutter. It is a Bible with a leather cover.)*

Hey, Donny — what's this Bible doing up here?

DONNY. I think it was a wedding gift.

BUCK. *(Inspecting the pages.)* Hasn't ever been opened.

DONNY. Maybe *that* was our problem. *(Donny works, as Buck pages through the Bible.)*

BUCK. I buried Grace with hers, you know. She asked me to do that. (Probably 'cause she knew I'd never read it.) I wrapped it in her Boston Red Sox pennant, tucked it in beside her, and watched them close the lid. *(Looking down at the Bible.)* Haven't held one since.

DONNY. You're welcome to that one.

BUCK. You don't think Rita wants it? *(Donny just stares at him — then goes back to work.)* How is Rita?

DONNY. She's in Italy.

BUCK. *(Pause, with caution.)* With that ... guy?

DONNY. *Cale.* Yes, she's in Italy with *Cale.* They're cheek to cheek in some gondola, throwing coins at the stinkin' canals.

BUCK. It's her life, Donny.

DONNY. I know that — all right? — *I know that.* But this guy, Buck — this *Cale* — I mean, PLEASE — what is she *thinking?*

BUCK. It's an *adjustment,* Donny — this is my point. I wake up one day and boom: my son is a cheerleader and my daughter is a cop. You wake up and boom: you're all alone and your wife is dating *lettuce.* It's weird stuff, Donny. It's through-the-looking-glass kinda stuff — *(Trisha bursts into the room, out of breath, her arms overflowing with a variety of objects from her childhood: dolls, books, clothes, a stickhorse, a plastic guitar, etc. She stands, staring at Donny — who slowly rises and looks at her, the room between them.)*

DONNY. *(Quietly.)* Hi, honey.

TRISHA. Dad. *(Silence.)*

DONNY. Listen, I want to explain why I —

TRISHA. *(Simply.)* Please don't talk right now.

DONNY. Trisha —

TRISHA. *Dad.* I made you some walnut cookies. I was at my friend Angel's house and we were bored and we started to bake things and I made you some cookies — walnut, the way you like them —

DONNY. Thank you.

TRISHA. And they're really bad, but I —

17

DONNY. No, I'm sure they're —

TRISHA. Trust me, Dad. They're bad. *Deeply* bad. But, you know — "thought that counts" and all that — I put 'em in a jar and decided to bring 'em over to you this morning.

And I get here. And people I don't know are sitting on the lawn looking at my baby pictures. There's an old woman wearing my Donald Duck mask and three guys are fighting over my junior high bowling trophy. I start to grab my things away from people and they're all like "First Come, First Served" and I'm like "THIS IS MY HOME, THESE ARE MY THINGS" — and pretty soon I had gone kind of what you would call *ballistic* and I was shoving people and grabbing at everything I could, but they just kept *swooping back* and filling up their cars, until there was nothing left but old socks and coat hangers and music from the seventies. *(In one motion, she drops everything she is holding to the ground, revealing one item that we have not previously seen: a glass jar filled with cookies.)* And my cookies. Nobody took *them*. *(She extends the jar of cookies toward Donny.)* So, here. *(Donny walks to her and takes the jar in his hand. She speaks to him — part anger, part concern.)* I don't know what you're doing, Dad. But, whatever it is, I don't like it. And, right now, I don't very much like *you*.

DONNY. Trisha, listen —

TRISHA. And I *mean it*, Dad. They're really bad. *(Trisha is gone, slamming the door shut behind her. Silence, as Donny stares at the cookies.)*

BUCK. You didn't even tell Trish? *(Donny stares at Buck, then begins to gather up the things Trisha has dropped to the ground. He places them, with care, inside a weathered red wagon. He also places the jar of cookies in a safe and prominent place in the room — perhaps on a small shelf on the upstage wall.)* So, what now? Once your house is empty and your stuff is gone — what then?

DONNY. *(Points to a place on the [unseen] ceiling.)* I'm gonna rip out that insulation and uncover the skylight. I'm gonna bring my old E-Z-Boy recliner in from the shed. I'm gonna lie back and look at the sky. And on the day after Trisha's birthday, I'm outta here.

BUCK. *(Still trying to make sense of it.)* Donny, what in the world —

DONNY. Every day for twenty years I worked on the surveying crew — me and Louise standing out in some field, taking readings

18

— and what did that *mean*? What does that add up to?

BUCK. It's your work, Donny, it's your —

DONNY. During that same twenty years there was a spacecraft — and while I was standing in those fields, this craft travelled six-point-two billion miles through space. *(A reverie.)* Pioneer Ten — the first object of human design to travel beyond our solar system. And now ... just like me ... its productive days are behind it.

BUCK. Donny — what kind of talk is —

DONNY. With its power ebbing, its signal feeble, Pioneer Ten is being officially retired. It will be set free of its orbit — allowed to drift silently through space for a million years. And do you know how many stars it will pass in a million years of travelling?

BUCK. Hundreds? Thousands?

DONNY. *Ten.* That's the enormity of it. The infinite promise.

BUCK. *(Pause.)* You're telling me you want to drift away somewhere?

DONNY. *(Simply.)* Too many years looking at the land, Buck. It's time to go higher. *(Silence, as Donny looks up and out of the skylight. Buck considers this. Then, finally —)*

BUCK. You know ... the phrase "*mid-life*" scares a lot of people. But in my mind, I —

DONNY. That's not what this is, Buck —

BUCK. *(Overlapping.)* — In my mind, I think it means the search for a new challenge. A new *project* of some kind. I mean, sure, we all have regrets — we all walk right past our "other life" every day of the year. Rita never opened her cafe, you never designed those parks and gardens you always talked about, and I never developed a taste for beer. But, small victories do happen, Donny —

DONNY. *(Busying himself once again.)* I don't need to hear a —

BUCK. When I turned forty, I decided to build a stone fence. Figured I'd get the rocks cleared off our half-acre — and end up with a little privacy from our nosenheimer neighbors. But, the first day out haulin' rocks, I overdid it — wrenched hell out of my back and damn near stopped my heart. Grace laid down the law: if I wanted that fence, I had to do it slowly ... *one stone each week.* Period. So, that's what I've been doing, Donny —

DONNY. You're still — ?

BUCK. — Even after Grace died, I kept my word. Every week I

go out and I add one stone to that fence. I'm twelve years into it ... and its about four feet long. By the time I finally get my privacy I won't *need any*. But, the point is: it's a *project*, Donny — it gives me something to —

DONNY. Go home, Buck. I don't need your help.

BUCK. *(Sharp.) You are not a spacecraft.* You have family and friends and responsibilities. You don't get to just *float away* — believe me, Donny, it's something I've been studying and it's not as simple as it sounds. Now, grab your coat and let's get some lunch —

DONNY. I'm not leaving, Buck.

BUCK. Well, I don't think you should be alone right now —

DONNY. I won't. Louise is coming by.

BUCK. *Good.* That's good. She's a fine woman, Donny. Always thought you and Louise'd do real well together, if you'd —

DONNY. Lou is my *friend*, Buck.

BUCK. — If you'd find a way to *overcome your friendship.*

DONNY. Do you ever listen to yourself?

BUCK. I'm just sayin', to a couple surveyors the fastest distance between two points is a *straight line*, am I right?

DONNY. *(Firm.)* Stop it.

BUCK. *(Pause.)* Is she still taking those night classes? Those religious-study-type classes?

DONNY. She's in the seminary, Buck.

BUCK. *(Holds up the Bible, looks at it.)* I should give her a call sometime. *(Donny has found something amid the stuff in the attic: a record album by Stan Getz and Joao Gilberto — weathered and faded, much played.)* What you got there?

DONNY. Just history. *(Donny wipes the dusty album with a rag.)* First time I heard this, thought I'd died and gone to heaven. Rita drug me into some hole-in-the-wall restaurant in Chinatown. It had a jukebox that looked like a trashed Pontiac. She threw a quarter into that machine and pushed a button. *(Speaks, a revery.)* "Quiet nights of quiet stars ..." *(Pause, quietly.)* "Corcovado." *(Donny leans the record album prominently against the jar of cookies from Trisha. Buck stares at him, worried, confused. Finally —)*

BUCK. Well. Thanks for the saw. It'll come in handy when I start my new project.

DONNY. Another fence?

BUCK. No. Something much *bigger* than a fence.

DONNY. *(Absently, returning to work.)* Well ... good luck.

BUCK. I'll need it, Donny. Believe me, we *all will. (Donny turns to Buck, curious about this remark, as — a few knocks are heard at the attic door.)*

DONNY. C'mon in, Lou. *(Rita enters. She looks great in her business attire. She carries a briefcase.)*

RITA. Hello, Donny. *(Donny stares at her, as does Buck.)*

DONNY. You're in Italy. Rita, you're supposed to be in Italy.

RITA. I was.

DONNY. You cut your trip short?

RITA. No.

DONNY. But, Rita, you told me —

RITA. We got back a week ago. Just like we planned. *(Silence, as Donny stares at her. Rita turns to Buck — who doesn't want to be there.)* How are you, Buck?

BUCK. Well, all in all, I'm —

DONNY. *(Still to Rita.)* Wait a minute. The *plan* — at least the one you told me — was that you'd get back a couple days before Trisha's birthday —

RITA. Right.

DONNY. — So you could make an appearance at the surprise party.

RITA. The one you've been planning for her.

DONNY. Right.

RITA. And remember how I doubted you, Donny? How I bet you couldn't truly surprise her? That you'd tip it off, somehow?

DONNY. Yes, I remember.

RITA. Well, I don't doubt you, anymore.

DONNY. I'm glad to hear that.

RITA. She was *very* surprised. When last Friday rolled around and *nothing happened* — it caught her *completely* off-guard.

DONNY. Wait —

RITA. She was so excited — clutching her new driver's license in her hand, hoping you'd let her drive your car to the restaurant. You know how much she loves your convertible. She sat like that for hours, waiting for you to *spring the big party on her.* Finally, at mid-

21

night, we ordered pizza and burned you in effigy. Well done, Donny. It's a surprise she'll never forget. *(Silence.)*

DONNY. *(Quietly.)* I lost a week. I lost a whole week.

RITA. Not from what I saw outside — looks like you put it to good use. Soon there won't be the slightest trace we were ever here.

DONNY. Rita, please, I'm —

RITA. *(Sharp.)* We had an *agreement*. Trisha would live with me, but you would keep this house for her, until she was grown — you would *keep things like they were* when she lived here.

DONNY. I tried to do that, Rita, but I —

RITA. The hell you did.

DONNY. Would you —

RITA. The *hell* you tried to do *anything* that took a little *effort*. As far as I can tell, we're *dead* to you, Donny. And, frankly, I don't mind it so much — but you've taken Trisha's heart and broken it in half.

DONNY. Would you please let me explain — ? *(A loud ringing sound. Donny stops, hearing it, trying to determine what it is, as — Rita opens her briefcase and removes a cellular phone.)* Rita, we're in the —

RITA. *(Abruptly.)* I have to take this.

BUCK. *(Seizing his chance to leave.)* And I have to go. I'll see you tomorrow.

DONNY. Buck — ? *(And Buck is gone, taking his Bible and saw with him. Donny turns to Rita, but she is speaking into the phone. He busies himself in the room, but gradually begins to listen to Rita's side of the conversation.)*

RITA. Yes? *(Pause, with genuine compassion.)* Hello, Mr. Mason. Yes, I'm afraid there is news and that it's not good. *(Pause, simply.)* We lost her. Yes. We did everything we could, but — *(Pause, quietly.)* Yes, I know. It's a great loss. I'm sorry. *(Pause, nods.)* If there's anything I can — *(Stops, pause.)* Yes. I'll tell them. *(Pause.)* You take care, now. *(Pause.)* Goodbye. *(Rita turns the phone off and stands quietly, motionless in the room. Donny finally asks —)*

DONNY. Someone we knew?

RITA. Hmm?

DONNY. Who passed away. Did we know them?

RITA. It's confidential, Donny.

22

DONNY. It's *what?*

RITA. When we have a loss, we're not allowed to discuss it — except with the registered user of the system.

DONNY. The *what?*

RITA. The most brutal part is that nine times out of ten it was their *own fault* — and *they know it*. They didn't make hard copies. They crashed the system even though they knew its limits. The technicians do everything they can to retrieve the data. But, if they fail ... that's where we come in.

DONNY. "We" who?!

RITA. The Data Recovery Counselors — it's what I'm doing now. We help users work through the anger and grief associated with loss.

DONNY. *(Incredulous.)* With loss of *things on their computers?!*

RITA. *(Holds up the phone.)* That man lost *everything*, Donny. Twelve gigabytes of data. His life's work — irretrievable — floating away in the ether. Can you imagine? Losing everything you'd built your life around? *(Donny stares at her, pointedly.)* Oh, please. Let's not dredge it all up again.

DONNY. Thought you'd had your fill of cyberspace. Last time we talked, it sounded like you were finally ready to open your cafe.

RITA. *(Holding up the phone.)* Donny, I talked a guy off a ledge last week. I was the only one he'd trust. I talked him back into the arms of the firemen. They kept him under observation for a few days, then released him.

DONNY. Well, that's —

RITA. Two days later, he hung himself. Some people, Donny, aren't ready to part with their things. *(She begins to move about the room, seeing/lifting things she recognizes —)* So, what are you doing?

DONNY. I'm not one of your patients, Rita. You can't change things by making me talk about it.

RITA. Yeah — we found *that* out, didn't we? *(Rita discovers a photo album. She sits and looks through it. Donny returns to his work.)*

DONNY. I'm sorry about the birthday.

RITA. She's dating now, you know.

DONNY. She didn't call it "dating" when I talked to her. She said they go to the mall with their friends.

RITA. This just in, Donny: Earth Not Flat. *She's dating.*

DONNY. What's his name again? "Wedge" or "Scrap" or —

23

RITA. *Shim.* His name is Shim.

DONNY. *Shim?! Cale?!* Who the hell *comes up with these?!*

RITA. *(Smiles a bit.)* Don't worry about Trisha. Her heart's in the right place.

DONNY. It's where her *body* is that I'm worried about.

RITA. She's a lot smarter than we were at that age, Donny.

DONNY. I was smart enough to find you.

RITA. *(Pause, gently.)* Don't. All right? *(She stands. During the following, she puts the photo album into her briefcase.)* I should go. I just stopped by to tell you that you were a bad father and ask why you were throwing away your life. So ... you know ... give me a call, sometime.

DONNY. I gave away my phone.

RITA. Suit yourself. *(They stand in silence, the room between them.)*

DONNY. *(Quietly.)* Rita —

RITA. You want it made simple, Donny. But what we did — the way things turned out — that doesn't get made simple. *(Pause.)* This was the Year of Being Real. Back in January, my friends and I were talking about New Year's resolutions — and we dared each other to do it: to spend a year in which we actually told everyone *exactly* what we thought of them, good or bad. No more white lies, no more keeping up appearances. A full year of putting the cards on the table. *(Pause.)* And now three of us are divorced. Two others left the country. We all changed jobs. And none of us are friends.

DONNY. Was it worth it?

RITA. I don't know. But it was necessary. You said so yourself. You said it was time to move on.

DONNY. I did say that.

RITA. Well?

DONNY. And then I spent a year trying to pretend that nothing had changed. That you hadn't decided to leave. That you were still here folding the towels the wrong way.

RITA. Donny —

DONNY. I even made plans for the honeymoon we never had.

RITA. Don't do this —

DONNY. What the hell were we *thinking:* not having a honeymoon?! Putting it off ("just a year or so" we both said) till we had more money or time or whatever-the-hell-we-thought-we-didn't-have-enough-of?!

RITA. It made sense. We were going to —

DONNY. *Sense?!* Nineteen years later — *divorced* — and *still no honeymoon* does not make *sense! (Going to her, fervently.)* I think there's a *window*, Rita. For everything in our lives, there's a window of time when it *must happen.* And if we let that window close —

RITA. You're making it sound —

DONNY. — Then we don't get it *back.* That chance is *gone.*

RITA. *(Firmly.)* Yes. It is. *(Silence. He stares at her.)*

DONNY. I found some books of yours. From your undergrad days, I think. *(He retrieves a vintage-style suitcase. Opens it.)* I put them in that [this] suitcase. Philosophy books, mainly. I always wondered why you saved them.

RITA. They might do you some good. Instead of behaving this way —

DONNY. And what way is that?

RITA. Foolishly — like your life is some kind of joke.

DONNY. *(With passion.)* "All great deeds have a ridiculous beginning."

RITA. *(Looking around.)* So, is this your *great deed?!* Is that what you're saying?

DONNY. Yes, it is. *(Donny quickly removes a book [Camus: The Myth of Sisyphus] from the suitcase and reads from it.)*

RITA. Donny, you're not making any sense —

DONNY. *"One day, in the midst of a man's life, the 'WHY' arises"* — and once it does, Rita — once the word "why" appears — at that moment *"everything begins."*

RITA. And what happens, Donny?

DONNY. A man either retreats into the dull habits of his life ... or he has an *awakening.*

RITA. So, do it. Set up your studio and do your work. Where's your drafting table? Your landscape books? Did you throw them away with the rest of us?

DONNY. Rita —

RITA. *(Sharp.)* Don't bring this up if you can't pursue it.

DONNY. When you were in grad school, you had a Psychology professor — third year, maybe —

RITA. Don't change the sub —

25

DONNY. I'm not — this professor gave your class an assignment. He asked you to write your own obituaries. Do you remember that?

RITA. Vaguely —

DONNY. As an exercise in self-awareness. To see how you'd truly like your life — the *totality* of your life — to be perceived, to be remembered. Did you ever do it, Rita?

RITA. If I did, I don't remember —

DONNY. I did it. Last week. Sitting in this attic. I took out a piece of paper and I wrote my obit: *(Gestures, as though it's a newspaper headline.)* "Donny Rowan, insert age of death. Never Went on a Honeymoon."

RITA. Donny —

DONNY. *(Overlapping.)* "Never Refinished His Attic." "Never Became the Great Landscape Architect of Our Time." "Never Threw a Surprise Party for His Daughter." "Always Just Stood There Pushing the 'Walk' Button."

RITA. *(Overlapping.)* Okay, stop it —

DONNY. "Never Asked his Wife to *Come Back.*" *(Long silence. Donny stares at Rita, then looks away. He moves to the suitcase and closes it.)* It's a joke, Rita. Like you said — it's all a big *joke.* Thanks for coming by. Take anything you want from the lawn — no charge. And tell Cale I said *"hi."* *(Rita looks at him. He moves away. She walks to the door, taking the suitcase and her briefcase with her. She stops. Donny turns back to her, saying —)* Rita ... *(Rita tosses Donny her cell phone. He catches it.)*

RITA. Call Trisha. You owe her that. *(Rita turns and is gone.)*

Scene 2

Dusk. The same day. The room is nearly cleared out. A hand-
ful of lamps and boxes remain, along with a vintage survey-
ing transit on a tripod — which is covered by an old blanket
or sheet. The jar of cookies and the record album remain
prominent in the room. Also: a small, square section of the
attic wall near the power outlet has been removed — revealing
an electrical cable which now protrudes from the opening.
One of the strands of the cable is wired to the now-exposed
electrical outlet. The other strand is hanging from the wall,
loose, exposed. Finally: another wire runs from this opening
to a single, aged stereo speaker which sits in a corner of the
room. The lights are off in the room. The door is closed. Light
from the hallway shines, as before, under the attic door. Also,
a shaft of the fading sunlight comes through the now-uncov-
ered skylight, landing on —

Louise, curled up on the ground amid a few of the boxes,
asleep. Donny and Buck emerge, carrying the recliner into
the attic. The recliner is fully covered with an old tarp of
some kind, which is fastened around the recliner with a
bungee cord. Donny and Buck — talking as they carry the
chair — do not immediately see Louise. She does not stir.

BUCK. But if you had to choose, Donny — if you had to choose
a couple people — well, *two,* let's say *two people* — to accompany
you on a — well — a *trip,* let's call it a *trip* — if you had to do
that, who would you choose? What two people?
DONNY. Buck, what — ?
BUCK. I am *taking stock,* Donny. Wouldn't hurt you to do the
same. A man must take stock — and then take action. *(Donny sets*
his side of the chair down. He plugs in the bundle of extension cords
— and the light of the lamps fills the room.) You can't fix your life

27

by giving it away.

DONNY. "Fix my life" — is that what you —

BUCK. You can't *rid yourself of yourself.*

DONNY. That's not what I'm —

BUCK. One trip. Two people. Name them. *(Donny gestures to where he wants the recliner placed. They move the chair as they speak.)*

DONNY. *(Relents.)* Trisha.

BUCK. That's one.

DONNY. This is foolish, Buck. I mean, what's the point of — *(Buck is staring at him, as they put the chair in place.)* You. Okay? *You.* Are you happy now?

BUCK. What about Louise?

DONNY. Okay, *Louise.* How's that? Trisha and Louise. Are we done now?

BUCK. And *Rita?*

DONNY. Well — sure — depending on — Buck, what the hell are you —

BUCK. It's not easy, is it? *(Donny has now seen Louise, sleeping.)*

DONNY. Ssshhh —

BUCK. That's what I'm finding out, Donny — when push come: to shove, it's not that easy to choose — *(Buck stops, because Donny is pointing to Louise, sleeping. They speak in a whisper, looking at her.)*

DONNY. Seminary.

BUCK. Must be hell.

DONNY. She's in the field all day and taking classes every night.

BUCK. So, when she graduates from there — *what is she?*

DONNY. What do you —

BUCK. Is she a minister or a priest or just a sort of — you know — Holy Person?

DONNY. You'll have to ask her yourself, Buck. *(Donny moves away and removes the Walk Signal from its box. A long electrical cord — with exposed wire — is now attached to the back of it. During the following, Donny connects this wire to the wire protruding from the attic wall.)*

BUCK. *(Looking down at Louise.)* She adores you, Donny. You must know that. It's clear as a new TV. *(Donny looks at Buck, then returns to his work.)* There's a tether, you know. Between people. A cord. And you and me — well, we get along all right. We laugh

28

together and come through for each other in a pinch. But, I think you could do without me, Donny. *(Pause.)* Louise, though ... well ... there's a tether between you. A bond. *(Donny — having attached the wire — looks down at Louise.)*

DONNY. We should go down and let her sleep.

LOUISE. *(Wide awake, eyes still closed.)* Oh, I wish I could. *(Donny and Buck look down at her.)* I would give *anything.* If I could — just once — *sleep.* All through the night, all through the changing numbers on the clock radio, all through the shadows moving on the walls and the thousand sounds from the house and the street ... all the way ... all the way till *morning. (A sigh, a pause.)* To do *that* — *just once* — I would eat glass, I would shave my head, I would burn my diaries, I would give away my car, I would drink shampoo, I would worship ants, I would donate my thumbs, I would marry another lawyer, I would stand naked on my roof and sing "Feelings," ANYTHING — if it meant *one true night's sleep. (Pause, opens her eyes.)* Oh, *great.* Now, I'm *awake.*

DONNY. *(Smiles.)* Hi, Lou.

LOUISE. Your lawn is nearly picked clean. All I could grab was this old sailor's cap. *(Louise pulls the cap — navy blue, wool, Greek fisherman's style — out from under her.)*

BUCK. *(Envious.)* I *knew* I should've taken it when I had a chance.

LOUISE. I had to have it, Buck. My ex had one just like this.

BUCK. I thought Bruce was a lawyer.

LOUISE. A lawyer with the heart of a sailor. (Not the brave, adventuresome part. More the *girl-in-every-port* part.) After the divorce, I gave Bruce everything. *Big mistake.*

DONNY. Why?

LOUISE. With no trace of him in that house — I forget how badly he treated me. From time to time I start to think, hey, it wasn't all so bad. My common sense turns to mush ... I get weak ... I reach for the phone ... *(Holds up the hat, squeezing it tightly.)* So, I *need this.* I need to *remember.*

DONNY. You told me it was the best thing you ever did — getting rid of all your stuff. *(Looking around the room.)* I took your advice to heart.

LOUISE. Well, live and learn, huh?

BUCK. I got a cat. *(They turn to him.)* When Grace died. I went

29

out and got a cat.

DONNY. I didn't know that.

BUCK. I hardly see it. It comes in and eats. Goes out and ... does whatever cats do, I guess. Once a year I box it up and take it to the vet for some shots.

DONNY. What did you name it?

BUCK. Name it? I hardly ever *see* it.

DONNY. That's odd, Buck — I took you for a dog person.

BUCK. I see a lot of animals in my future, Donny. *(Donny stares at him, blankly, then re-checks the cord he has just wired.)*

LOUISE. I could never own a cat.

BUCK. You allergic?

LOUISE. No. I couldn't stand to watch it *sleep all the time.*

BUCK. *(Referring to the now-wired Walk Signal.)* What's the plan there, Donny? Where'd you get that?

DONNY. You said I needed a light switch. *(A phone begins ringing. They all freeze for a moment, then Donny realizes it's coming from Rita's cell phone — which he finds inside an old picnic basket in the room. Donny opens the picnic basket, removes the phone and answers it.)*

LOUISE. When'd you get a cell phone?

DONNY. *(Into phone.)* Hello? *(Very pleased to hear her voice.)* Trisha — hi — it's me. Yeah — she gave me her phone. Listen, please don't hang up, I've been calling you all day, I want to — hold on a second — *(To Buck and Louise.)* I'll be downstairs. *(He speaks into the phone as he exits —)* I really need to see you, Trisha. Maybe you can stop by later and we can ... *(Donny is gone. Louise turns to Buck.)*

LOUISE. So, what's he told you?

BUCK. The chair. The skylight. The stars. That's it.

LOUISE. Not *why?*

BUCK. We're guys, Louise. "Why" is not standard equipment.

LOUISE. Oh, don't go there, Buck —

BUCK. Don't go where?

LOUISE. Behind the Guy Curtain. Back where the Wizard lives — secretly controlling your thoughts and emotions. Don't go there, okay? I'm wise to it.

BUCK. It's *real,* though, Louise, what I'm saying is —

LOUISE. I *know* it's real. I've seen the men in my life do it for years. You go behind the Guy Curtain and say "Oh, I don't really know him." "I can't really tell him how I feel" — because, hey, we're *guys*, we just put on our pants, eat our food and die.

BUCK. Louise, look —

LOUISE. This is not judgement, Buck. This is *envy*. It's incredible: If a guy likes another guy, he calls him up every now and then. If he doesn't like him, he *don't*. And the amazing thing is: the other guy *understands this completely*. He doesn't count the days between phone calls, he doesn't sit and wonder what tiny slight brought about this change in the status quo, he doesn't *keep score at all*. He just ... *calls some other guy*. It's so DIRECT it feels ... BARBARIC.

BUCK. Between me and Donny it's not so direct. At least not lately. There's something I haven't been able to tell him. *(Buck closes the door to the attic.)* I thought I might tell you, Louise. I thought you — of all people — might be able to shed some light on it for me.

LOUISE. I'll do what I can, Buck. *(He looks at her. Nods. Silence.)*

BUCK. Well, the thing is — and this is going to sound like I'm one pin shy of a spare, I warn you — but, the thing is ... I've been hearing voices. Well, *one voice*, I guess. Someone's been speaking to me, Louise. At first the voice came from my TV — so I shut it off ... but the voice continued. So I put my TV in the shed and the voice stopped. I thought that was the end of it. Then, one morning, the voice came from my fridge. So, I started eating out. In time, it's come from my medicine chest, my telephone, my mailbox, my sock drawer — it's EVERYWHERE, Louise. *(Pause.)* And I wanted to talk to you because I think I know who it is. *(Pause.)* I think it's God. *(Silence.)*

LOUISE. *(Trying to be helpful.)* And why do you think it's God, Buck?

BUCK. Well ... he's asking me to do something. Something that I think God would ask someone to do — I mean, you know, based on what we know or have been told of God and what — from time to time — he asks someone to I must be totally out of my mind.

LOUISE. *(Going to him.)* Let's say you're not, Buck. Let's say there is a voice. And that maybe it's God's.

BUCK. Has he talked to *you?*

31

LOUISE. No. But, I'm hopeful. I spend a lot of time at the seminary trying to imagine what that would be like, you know?

BUCK. I *do* know. And, believe me, it can be frightening — but I keep telling myself: we have nothing to fear but the fear of ourselves.

LOUISE. So, he's asking something of you?

BUCK. Yes, he is.

LOUISE. He wants you to do something for him?

BUCK. Yes.

LOUISE. And what is that?

BUCK. He wants me to build an ark. *(Silence. Louise just stares at him.)*

LOUISE. That's been done, Buck.

BUCK. I guess this is the *sequel.* He won't say *why* exactly, because, well, we don't really have *conversations* — I just walk around my house waiting for inanimate objects to speak to me.

LOUISE. I see.

BUCK. So, I wondered — knowing God, or at least studying him as you do — I wondered what you thought of all this.

LOUISE. Has he mentioned, you know ... *when?*

BUCK. Actually, he's pretty short on specifics — which surprised me.

LOUISE. Not how big the ark should be, what species should be saved?

BUCK. From what I can tell, it's a little more *free-form* this time. He's kind of — and, well, this is the part that makes me a little nervous — he's kind of leaving it up to me.

LOUISE. Really?

BUCK. Yeah — and I pave roads for a living — what do I know about driving a boat and saving mankind?! But, he doesn't seem worried. *(Removing a small notebook from his pocket.)* The only advice he gave me is: *lists.* Make a lot of *lists.* Then, I choose whoever seems worthy, load 'em up and wait for rain. *(A pause. Then, Louise smiles warmly.)*

LOUISE. Wouldn't it be great, Buck? If we truly had a threat like that looming over us — something that forced us to make a new start.

BUCK. Well, in fact, I think we —

LOUISE. I sit in class at night. And my professor is talking about

32

redemption. The gift of God's grace. And as I'm filling my spiral notebook with these vague and lovely words, my thoughts drift away and out the window. And from where I sit ... everything is a light. The cars. The street. The buildings. And beyond them, the stars. Each and every one a light. And I sit there and wonder how He finds me. One speck of light amid the rest — yet somehow, through prayer, through faith, He finds me. Or, I *believe* he does. And, my life is the tension between that which I see ... and that which I believe.

BUCK. *(Pause.)* You think I'm making it up.

LOUISE. No, I don't. We *are* responsible — we *all* have choices to make. What to abandon and what to save.

BUCK. Yeah, but I've got to build a boat.

LOUISE. *(Smiles.)* It's a metaphor, Buck. It represents the things you —

BUCK. But the *voices,* Louise — what about the —

LOUISE. You're a perceptive man. Your mind is in touch with these thoughts, these fears. Most people can't face them, they learn to block them out, but you've —

BUCK. He asked me to save Bruce. *(Silence.)*

LOUISE. I must have misheard you. I thought you said —

BUCK. It's the only person he mentioned by name. Isn't that odd? Everyone else is up to me to choose, but he specifically mentioned Bruce.

LOUISE. My Bruce?

BUCK. Yes.

LOUISE. My skirt-chasing, tax-cheating, compulsively lying ex-husband LAWYER?!

BUCK. Look, maybe it's like you said. Maybe it's just my imagination —

LOUISE. Did he mention *me?*

BUCK. *(Pause.)* Let's not get into this now —

LOUISE. You've got to be kidding! He wants you to save — *(Stops, pause.)* This, Buck, is what they call a "test of faith." *(Buck approaches Louise. He opens his small notebook, and shows it to her, saying —)*

BUCK. You're on my list, Louise. I want you to know that.

LOUISE. Thank you. *(Donny enters, as — Louise speaks more*

brightly, aware of Donny's presence.) I mean, not that it's really *possible*, not that it could actually —
BUCK. Right. Of course not.
LOUISE. It's just a fantasy. Your mind playing tricks.
BUCK. Right. *(Pause, lifts the notebook.)* But, even so.
LOUISE. *(Nods.)* Right.
DONNY. What are you talking about?
BUCK. I'll stop by later, Donny. Got to put my new saw to use.
DONNY. Take something down, would you?
BUCK. No problem. *(Buck picks up a box or container. He looks down inside it as he starts off. He stops. He removes a large, black umbrella from inside the box. He hands it to Donny, saying —)* I'd hold onto this. *(Buck leaves. Donny holds the umbrella, watching him go.)*
DONNY. I worry about him, Lou.
LOUISE. *Don't.* He'll be fine. *(Louise moves about the attic, looking around.)*
DONNY. Was he asking about … *(Gestures "you and me" repeatedly.)* … you know.
LOUISE. Hmm?
DONNY. It's just that he never stops. Asking me about … *(Gestures "you and me" again. Louise does the identical gesture back at Donny.)* You know what I mean.
LOUISE. And what do you say?
DONNY. Louise —
LOUISE. Right. Got it. Let's not go there — that might lead to actual emotion. *(She pulls the covering off the vintage surveying transit.)* I wondered if you'd kept this. It's a relic now, in the days of lasers. Pretty soon *we'll* be relics. We'll be statues in the Civil Engineer Theme Park.
DONNY. We've been through this, Louise, we've *had* this discussion — *(Louise spins the transit on its base and "points" it at Donny. She looks at him through the eyepiece, as she speaks.)*
LOUISE. "Asked and answered," right? That's what Bruce would say. "Asked and answered" — let's move on.
DONNY. Don't compare me to Bruce.
LOUISE. You give me no choice. You view a conversation we had years ago as a solid object — something that time can't change. But,

34

people aren't buildings, Donny. They are liquid. Life is motion.

DONNY. Is that Seminary-Speak? *(She stares at him, hard.)* Sorry.

LOUISE. What ever happened to your Great Work? That's what we called it, didn't we? The work you were going to do in this attic. You were going to set up your studio here — *(Points to various parts of the room.)* your drafting table — the lamp above it — your photos — your books ... and you were going to design landscapes. City parks, country gardens. You were going to stop measuring the land and start shaping it. *(Pause.)* It was a good dream, Donny.

DONNY. You're *direct*, Lou. I'll give you that.

LOUISE. Why don't you give me an answer, instead?

DONNY. My "Great Work" — what arrogance. It's laughable now —

LOUISE. You studied, you planned, you started to turn this room into your —

DONNY. I started a lot of things, Lou. What matters, is I didn't *finish* any of them.

LOUISE. Do it now. Now that the clutter is gone: *Finish something.* I'll help you, Donny. We'll get your drafting table up here and —

DONNY. I gave it away —

LOUISE. Put a door across some boxes — it doesn't matter — just *do your work.*

DONNY. Louise —

LOUISE. Oh, am I out of line, here? Well, don't have friends then. Because that's what friends do: They lie awake at night — in my case, *nearly all night*, which makes me a remarkable friend — and they put other people's lives in order. "If only he'd do this and that and that — everything would be fine. It's so simple — why can't he see that?" Nothing is more obvious than the solutions to our friends' problems. *(Smiles.)* So, please, Donny, it's *time*: do what I think's best for you.

DONNY. I think there's a parallel world, Lou. And maybe somewhere, in that parallel world, I am doing just that — I am at a drafting table, the pencil moving my arm like water. And I am designing a landscape. *(Silence, as she studies him.)*

LOUISE. You think in a parallel world everything is *perfect*? You think it all works out?

DONNY. Don't you?

LOUISE. Absolutely not. I think we all make the same mistakes in new and interesting ways.

DONNY. But what about your faith — the place you call "heaven"?

LOUISE. What I call heaven is a place where you can always get a *full night's sleep* and a *really good piece of pie*. Small-minded of me, I know. But where is God if not in our senses? In our sights and smells and tastes. Those are the details, Donny, and He is there.

DONNY. *(Looking up at the skylight.)* And beyond that? Beyond those details, what is out there?

LOUISE. *(Simply, honestly.)* I don't know. *(Pause.)* Do you? *(He turns and looks at her.)* Is that where your future is? On the other side of that skylight? Because I thought it was right here, in this room. I saw your portfolio, you know. I saw the work you were starting to do.

DONNY. It was nothing. It amounts to —

LOUISE. It's up here somewhere, isn't it? I bet it is —

DONNY. Stop it, Lou —

LOUISE. I bet it's still lying around up here — *(Louise begins rummaging through the remaining things in the attic.)*

DONNY. It's gone, Louise. It was crap — all of it. The whole idea — it was a pipe dream. It's long gone. *(Louise discovers a [previously unseen] large, weathered leather portfolio.)*

LOUISE. Really? It looks like you saved it. If it's no good, why are you saving it?

DONNY. I'm *not*, all right?! It's going to the dump with everything else no one wants.

LOUISE. *(Firmly.)* Don't speak for me. Don't tell me what I want. *(She sets the portfolio down near her.)* You're lucky to have found Rita. I hope you know that. I wouldn't have been as patient, Donny. I would have harangued you day and night — till you set up your studio and did your work. *(Donny approaches her, stands very close to her.)*

DONNY. Maybe I needed you to do that.

LOUISE. It's not too late, Donny. *(Donny takes hold of her arms, looks in her eyes. Louise clarifies her statement ...)* For your *work*. *(Pause.)* As for us ... I've put that thought away —

DONNY. But time changes it, you said so yourself —

LOUISE. *(Moving away.)* But the thing is, Donny: It doesn't change *you*. Your picture of me is *fixed*, frozen in time. We're buddies, Donny. Partners on the surveying crew. And do you know what that means? Our life, like our work, is based on the *distance between us*. *(Pause.)* So, I do what I've always done: I mourn the part of your life you won't give me ... and I love the rest.

DONNY. *(Starts toward her.)* Louise —

LOUISE. *(She stops him with a raised hand, speaks quietly.)* They tell me only a tragedy will make me sleep. *(A wry smile.)* A grand prescription, don't you think? The last specialist I went to told me that my only hope — outside a life of pills and more pills — is a severe shock to my system. Something that takes my life and turns it inside out, casting all smaller questions aside. Only then, he said, will my body finally give over to sleep. *(She goes to him.)* Finish it, Donny. Put things in order up here and do your work. Will you promise me that?

DONNY. *(Pause, simply.)* I will. *(She stares at him. Then she gives him a tender kiss on the cheek — and leaves, taking the portfolio with her. Donny looks at the room. He goes to the door and closes it. He brings the Walk Signal near the chair, setting it on a box. He removes the large tarp which has covered the chair. He looks up at the skylight. He moves the chair ever-so-slightly to improve the view. He moves the box accordingly — so he can reach the Walk Signal from his chair. Satisfied, he begins folding up the tarp. Pause. He looks at the door. Donny takes the folded up tarp and places it against the bottom of the door — blocking the space where light is leaking through. As he steps back into the room, the door opens, and — Trisha enters.)*

TRISHA. You said you wanted to see me.

DONNY. *(Going to her.)* Trisha, I've been calling you all day —

TRISHA. Yeah, that's what you said —

DONNY. Why didn't you —

TRISHA. I was real busy.

DONNY. I see.

TRISHA. Yeah, with school and going to the mall with Shim.

DONNY. How is Shim?

TRISHA. I don't get you, okay? You ask me things and I don't know why — because it doesn't seem like it even matters —

DONNY. Trisha —

TRISHA. What do you care what I've been doing? You don't even —

DONNY. I care, Trisha. I've failed to show you that lately, I know. But, over the past year, I don't know, I've —
TRISHA. Been going kind of crazy? That's what Mom says. She makes excuses for you. She hates to admit it, but she does. She says I should forgive you for missing my birthday.
DONNY. I'm sorry about that. I had every intention to —
TRISHA. Right. Whatever. I don't forgive you. *(Trisha sees the tarp near the base of the door.)* What's that for?
DONNY. It blocks the light. I want the room perfectly dark.
TRISHA. Why?
DONNY. Hmm?
TRISHA. Why do you want it dark? *(He stares at her.)*
DONNY. You hungry? I can see if there's something in the kitchen to —
TRISHA. You have spices and water. I checked.
DONNY. *(Lifting the jar of cookies she brought him.)* How 'bout a cookie?
TRISHA. *(More serious.)* I'm not a kid, Dad. You can't ignore my questions. *(Silence. He moves toward the recliner.)*
DONNY. Do you want to go for a ride?
TRISHA. Dad —
DONNY. I know you're not a kid, anymore — but when you were, I used to take you for rides in this chair. I'd sit you on my lap and we'd make up places — far away — and we'd travel to them.
TRISHA. That was a long time ago. I liked you then. *(She see the Walk Signal, lifts it.)* Did you steal this?
DONNY. Don't press that — I'm still wiring it.
TRISHA. What will it do?
DONNY. More than it did before. *(She sets it back down on the box. Donny gestures for her her to sit in the chair.)* I want to take you somewhere. Somewhere new.
TRISHA. I can't stay very —
DONNY. *(Desperately.)* Please. Grant me this one thing. *(Trisha looks at him, then sits in the chair, stiffly.)* You can lean back, you know.
TRISHA. I'm fine. *(During the following, Donny goes around to all the lamps in the room and, one by one, turns them off. He also closes the attic door.)*
DONNY. Have you heard of Hamlet?

TRISHA. Everyone's heard of Hamlet, Dad. He's always talking to that skull.

DONNY. Not that Hamlet. An earlier one. There is a Greek myth about a man who dropped a giant salt grinder to the bottom of the sea. He was called Hamlet — and his grinder was called Hamlet's Mill. And this mill has continued to grind, under the sea — for generations — and that's the reason —

TRISHA. That the ocean is salty?

DONNY. *(Smiles.)* Yes — very good — but something more. The motion of that grinding accounts for the wobble of the earth on its axis. *(Indicating it with a small lamp.)* His wobble, like a huge gyroscope, is very slight, very slow — it takes nearly 26,000 years for it to complete one full cycle.

TRISHA. Where did you learn all this stuff?

DONNY. It's research. For my trip. *(He turns off all but the final lamp in the room, as he speaks —)* And, the amazing thing is this: when that wobble is measured against the fixed stars — the *March equinox point* is actually, ever-so-slightly, *earlier* each year. Do you know what that means?

TRISHA. Time is going *backwards*?

DONNY. Exactly. It's called the "precession of the equinoxes." *(Trisha looks at him, then smiles a bit, as she makes the chair recline, getting more comfortable. Donny turns off the final lamp in the room. The only light in the room is the moonlight coming in through the skylight and illuminating Trisha in the chair — and the light from the hallway pouring in under the closed door.)*

TRISHA. Dad?

DONNY. Hmm?

TRISHA. The light. *(Trisha points to the "light leak" under the door. Donny nods and puts the tarp in place at the base of the door — fully blocking the light.)*

DONNY. How's that? *(Trisha looks up and out the skylight — enjoying the dark room and the moon above her.)*

TRISHA. *(Quietly.)* "The moon is my eye on you." *(Pause.)* You sent me a postcard once when I was little. Mom read it to me. "When I'm far away, remember this: the moon is my eye on you." *(Pause.)* You're going away, aren't you?

DONNY. *(Quietly.)* Yes.

TRISHA. Far away? *(He looks at her, saying nothing. He moves close to the chair and takes her hand. They each look up at the skylight as they speak.)* Let's say you're going to the edge of the universe. How far would that be?

DONNY. About fifteen billion light-years.

TRISHA. So, you'd never make it. You'd never live long enough to get there.

DONNY. Don't forget: once you leave the Earth's gravity, you accelerate. And the faster you travel, the more slowly time seems to pass.

TRISHA. Relativity.

DONNY. Very good. So, if your acceleration remains constant, by the time you reach the edge of the universe — fifteen billion light-years away — you've only aged about forty-seven years. *(Trisha looks up at the skylight, pleased by this thought.)*

TRISHA. So, it's possible.

DONNY. Theoretically. *(Pause.)* What's Cale like? *(Trisha looks at him, then stands. During the following, she walks around the room and turns all the lamps back on — one by one.)* I just wondered.

TRISHA. Why now? Why do you finally ask that now?

DONNY. I just wanted to —

TRISHA. You still love her, don't you?

DONNY. She's a great woman, Trish. A great and difficult woman.

TRISHA. Cale's the real thing, I think. For Mom. I think he's definitely the real thing.

DONNY. Unlike me, you mean.

TRISHA. Mom calls you her "Starter Husband." She says she's traded up.

DONNY. She probably has.

TRISHA. And she got Cale to stop smoking — which was a big deal, you know how Mom hates cigarettes.

DONNY. You think they'll get married?

TRISHA. I hope so. Otherwise she'll just have me. And I don't need the pressure of that.

DONNY. What do you need? What can I give you?

TRISHA. My birthday's over, Dad, if that's what this is about —

DONNY. I don't mean for your birthday.

TRISHA. But why, then — I don't get you —

DONNY. How about this? *(Donny holds up a key ring.)*

40

TRISHA. A car? *(Pause.)* You mean it?! *(He nods. He hands her the key ring.)* Dad, I can't believe you — *(She stops. Looks more closely at the keys.)* Wait. This is *your* car. Your convertible.

DONNY. Now, it's yours. *(She stares at him, thrilled, confused.)*

TRISHA. Really? *(Donny nods.)* Why?

DONNY. I want you to have it. Be safe — don't go anywhere your mom tells you not to — but enjoy yourself. You deserve it.

TRISHA. What are you going to drive?

DONNY. I'll figure something out. *(She stares at him, then impulsively hugs him. He holds her tightly, as he speaks to her.)* There's a second key on there. The smaller one.

TRISHA. Is that the glove compartment?

DONNY. No.

TRISHA. The gas tank? The trunk?

DONNY. It's for a box — a safety deposit box at the bank. I had it put in your name, Trish.

TRISHA. I don't underst —

DONNY. If you need anything — for any reason — after I've gone — go there and use that key. I've left things there for you.

TRISHA. *(Quietly.)* I don't want your *things*, Dad. I don't miss being around your *things*. I miss *you*. Where are you going?

DONNY. I'm not sure, Trisha. And that's the honest truth.

TRISHA. That's not *good enough*. You have to tell me something! You can't just —

DONNY. Trisha, listen: *(He takes her by the shoulders, looks into her eyes.)* Whatever is of value about me — you already have. It's *in you*. Through no fault of my own, you've become the absolute best part of me. And *nothing* can change that. Nothing I do can take that away from you. Do you understand?

TRISHA. *(Quietly, tears in her eyes.)* No.

DONNY. Will you try to? For me? Will you please *try*? *(Trisha nods. Then she pulls away, wiping her eyes.)*

TRISHA. I should go. Buck's waiting for me.

DONNY. He is?

TRISHA. He gave me a ride over. When did he start reading the Bible so much?

DONNY. No idea. *(Pause.)* You can take the car now, if you want.

TRISHA. *(Excited.)* Really?

DONNY. Have you driven at night, yet?

TRISHA. Once or twice.

DONNY. Have Buck follow you home, okay? *Remind him that I asked him to look after you.*

TRISHA. Okay. *(An aching silence. They stare at each other. Then, Trisha moves to the door.)*

DONNY. Take good care, Trisha.

TRISHA. *(Nods.)* Send me a postcard, okay? *(Pause.)* I love you, Dad. *(He steps toward her, but — She turns and is gone. Donny stares at the door for a long time … then he goes to the door and closes it. He slides the bolt, locking it. He replaces the tarp at its base, secures it, blocking the light. He turns back into the room and looks around. He walks to where the jar of cookies and record album are placed. He lifts the record album and looks at it. He opens the jar and takes out a cookie. Donny puts the cookie in his shirt pocket. He looks at the chair, at the skylight. Then … he moves to the chair and sits. He looks around the room once more. Then, he reclines back in the chair — preparing for his journey. He takes a long, deep breath … then, he pushes the Walk Signal button. When he does so — the lamps go out and the room is dark, except for the shaft of moonlight on Donny at the recliner, and, simultaneously — music plays: perhaps "Corcovado" — initially heard from the speaker in Donny's attic, and then filling the entire theatre, lushly.* And now … the walls of the attic gradually open out — or become translucent — revealing an endless vista of stars. Donny reclines in his chair, staring up at the skylight … a small man dwarfed by a multitude of heavenly bodies. A smile crosses his lips, as he takes another deep breath, and then — The amplified sound of very loud pounding at the locked attic door, is heard on tape. We hear Buck's [taped] voice shouting over the music —)*

BUCK'S VOICE. *(Urgent, frantic.)* DONNY! DONNY — OPEN UP! DONNY — ARE YOU IN THERE?! *(Donny does not react, as the — music swells, and the — light on Donny becomes blazingly white, and the — world of stars grows brighter and brighter, and then — a shooting star crosses the heavens, and — everything rushes to black.)*

---

* See Special Note on Songs and Recordings on copyright page.

ACT TWO

Loud music from the darkness. A shaft of light rises on Donny, standing in the exact place where the recliner had been. He wears a change of clothing. His head is tilted upward. His eyes are closed. Near him, at his feet, is an orange life preserver. Over the music, we again hear the sound of pounding on the locked attic door — identical to the end of Act One. And, as before, we hear Buck's [taped] voice —

BUCK'S VOICE. DONNY! DONNY — OPEN UP! DONNY — ARE YOU IN THERE?! (*A loud crash of a door being kicked into a room [also on tape] is heard, as — the music plays, and whatever scenic effect was used at the end of Act One is now reversed [if possible], bringing us from the expanse of space back into the reality of the attic. It is afternoon. The nearly empty attic is slightly altered, as follows: The recliner is gone. As is the Walk Signal. Also gone is the record album and the jar of cookies. The open patch in the wall is closed over, as before. The umbrella we saw Buck hand to Donny in Act One is open and sitting on the ground at center stage. An aged wooden ladder leans against a wall. A table, legs folded up, also leans against a wall. Two older, vintage suitcases are stacked in a corner.*
    Also: a telescope on a tripod now sits in the exact place where the surveyor's transit sat in Act One. It is covered in the identical manner as the transit. Finally: The door to the room lies on the floor, presumably having been knocked into the room. Buck stands in the doorway. His clothes are different than in Act One. He wears shorts, a colorful t-shirt, and a long, yellow rain slicker. On his head is the blue sailor's cap we saw in Act One. On his feet are galoshes. As the music ends, Buck approaches Donny slowly. Donny, eyes still closed, is not aware of him.)
BUCK. (*Whispers.*) Donny. (*No response.*) Donny, it's me.
DONNY. (*Simply, opening his eyes.*) Hey, Buck. How's things?
BUCK. You okay, Donny?

43

DONNY. Fine.

BUCK. I was worried that you didn't survive the journey.

DONNY. The what?

BUCK. I'm so glad we traveled together, Donny — believe me, you don't want to go through something like that alone. And sorry about your door, but I needed to tell you it's safe to come out now.

DONNY. Safe...?

BUCK. Man, what a ride! Got the ark built just in time. Got the last person loaded and boom: water covered the world like a blanket. I watched rivers swallow cities and oceans devour lakes. One hundred and fifty days, Donny — and I don't know about you, but I thought it would *never end.* Twice I released the dove into the air — and twice she returned, having found no place to alight. And then this morning — just on a hunch — I released her again (Have you noticed how these things always seem to happen in *threes?*) ... and she returned, Donny ... and there in her beak was this — *(He produces a tiny branch with a few leaves.)* an olive branch, plucked fresh from a tree. I threw open the doors, and there before us was the land — infinite and green, like a promise well-kept. *(With glee.)* The deluge is over, Donny, and we survived it! It's something we'll be able to tell our *parents and our grandparents* — and if you want to see the *rainbow to end all rainbows,* just take a look outside!

DONNY. Buck, let me get this straight. You're under the impression that — *(Rita enters. She wears jeans and a casual sweater. She also wears a cook's apron featuring the following words, prominently: The Off-Line. Rita goes directly to Donny — walking over the fallen door — as Buck says —)*

BUCK. Tell him, Rita. Tell Donny what — *(With no hesitation, Rita takes Donny's face in her hands and kisses him long and hard on the mouth. Then, she pulls back, takes a deep breath, and looks Donny in the eyes.)*

DONNY. How long's it been?

RITA. Three days, two hours and ten minutes.

DONNY. You're doing great. Keep it up.

BUCK. I can leave — you want me to leave?

RITA. No, I need to talk to you — *(Quickly.)* Damnit. *(She immediately takes Donny's face in her hands and kisses him, as before.)*

BUCK. *(Sits, removing his galoshes.)* Is that what getting younger does to you?

RITA. *(Pulling away, taking a deep breath)* It's our latest experiment.

DONNY. She's tried everything, you know — for years now — to stop smoking.

BUCK. Yeah, I remember that scary lady with the needles —

DONNY. And nothing's ever worked —

RITA. So, my new theory is very simple: every time I crave a cigarette — no matter where I am or what I'm doing — I kiss my husband, instead. Three days and counting.

BUCK. Yeah, but what's in it for Donny? *(Rita frowns playfully at Buck — and tosses her cook's apron to Donny.)*

RITA. Can you cover the counter for me? We got slammed at lunch, and I need a break. And tell Trisha to work the front tables.

DONNY. On her birthday?

RITA. Can't be helped. *(On his way downstairs, Donny lifts the fallen door and leans it against a wall, upstage.)* What happened to our door?

BUCK. I did. *(Donny goes, as — Rita goes to the umbrella, closes it, and hangs it somewhere in the room, during the following. Buck lifts the life-preserver and holds onto it.)* I wanted to tell Donny that the waters had receded.

RITA. Are you still on this Noah kick?

BUCK. Why is this so hard for everyone to believe?!

RITA. Because everything is just the same as it was yesterday when you said the world ended.

BUCK. Maybe it only *appears* to be the same. Maybe — in some real but quiet way — there has been *fundamental change. (Rita goes to him. Takes him by the shoulders. Looks him in the eyes.)*

RITA. Buck, listen to me —

BUCK. *(Moving away.)* If you want a cigarette, I'll go get Donny.

RITA. *(Kindly.)* This was charming when you were older. And we kept saying to ourselves: "It's a phase. He'll pass through it. When he gets a little younger, these delusions will pass." But, it's gone on too long, Buck. It's time to let it go.

BUCK. But, did you *see* that rainbow?

RITA. *(Simply.)* No, Buck — I didn't.

BUCK. You — *(Stops, pause.)* You didn't?

RITA. It hasn't rained in weeks. Wish it would — our garden is bone dry. *(Silence.)*

BUCK. But the *voices*, Rita —

RITA. *(Gently.)* Put them out of your mind. *(Pause.)* Now, I have a favor to ask. After Trisha's birthday, Donny and I are going on a trip. *(Buck hangs the life-preserver on the wall.)*

BUCK. He didn't mention anything about —

RITA. He doesn't know this, yet. I want to take him on a tour of all the landscapes he designed. He was a remarkable designer, Buck. He could take a piece of land and make it sing.

BUCK. Why did he give it up?

RITA. That's what I'm hoping to learn on this trip. And I need your help.

BUCK. You want to use my boat?

RITA. I want you to look after the cafe while we're gone. Can you do that?

BUCK. *(Excitedly.)* Absolutely. The Off-Line will be in good hands, Rita.

RITA. And you know the rules, right?

BUCK. No cell phones. No beepers. No laptops.

RITA. Very good.

BUCK. "When you come to the Off-Line, the world cannot find you."

RITA. You've got to *watch 'em like a hawk*, Buck. Not the regulars — they know the score. But the newcomers still have that fear of disengagement — they still believe there's a Big Call Coming and it will Come Once and Never Come Again. They're the ones who sneak the cell phone inside their socks.

BUCK. I got it covered, Rita. What time's the party tonight?

RITA. Seven.

BUCK. Does Trisha know?

RITA. Definitely not. We made sure it's a surprise. *(Trisha enters. Her clothes, too, are different than Act One — slightly more sophisticated. She is followed quickly by Donny — still wearing the off-Line apron.)*

TRISHA. *(Seemingly in one breath)* Angel can't come to my party — her mom's being a real jerk about it — and I don't want to turn sixteen without her — she's been my best friend since I was, like, *forty* — so can we do the party another night? — maybe next week, I'll have Angel check her schedule and then we can —

46

(Stops, looks at them.) Oh. Was I supposed to act surprised? *(Pause.)* Sorry. *(Trisha goes.)*

BUCK. Oh, well. You tried.

DONNY. *(With a smile.)* And she fell for it.

RITA. *(Smiling.)* Yes, she did. Let's put up the banner. *(During the following, Donny and Rita go to a corner of the room and remove a large banner from its hiding place. Buck watches them.)*

BUCK. Fell for what?

DONNY. You'll see, Buck. Don't worry.

BUCK. You never tell me *anything*. Just because I'm the *oldest*, you never —

RITA. Enjoy it while you can. *(They unfurl the banner, which reads: TRISHA — HAPPY 16th!. Rita speaks, wistfully.)* Sixteen — how did this happen? She's almost gone, Donny. Sixteen years left … and then she'll be history. She'll be photos in a book. *(Pause.)* What will we do when she's —

DONNY. *(Goes to her, holds her.)* Ssshhh. We'll be fine.

BUCK. You'll still have me.

RITA. *(Mock disdain.)* Great.

BUCK. *(Rubbing it in.)* Yep, *I'm old* — I'm gonna be around a long time.

RITA. *(Pulling away from Donny.)* I want to talk to her. *(The banner.)* Will you —

DONNY. Sure. *(Rita takes a few steps, then quickly says —)*

RITA. Damnit. *(— and immediately turns and kisses Donny on the mouth, then leaves.)*

BUCK. How've you done it, Donny? *(Buck helps Donny with the banner. Using the ladder, they hang the banner in the room during the following.)* You and Rita — all these years? What's the secret? Always talk things out? Never go to bed mad? Things like that?

DONNY. I just follow one simple rule, Buck.

BUCK. What's that?

DONNY. Do the opposite of what feels natural. When Rita and I hit a rough patch and I want nothing more than to just fold my arms, sit there and sulk — *I make myself say something, anything.* And whenever I really want to scream and yell — *I shut up.* Works every time.

BUCK. I'll keep that in mind.

DONNY. Something you want to tell me, Buck?

BUCK. *(The banner.)* Where do you want this?

DONNY. Do you have something to report?

BUCK. I don't know what you're —

DONNY. C'mon, Buck. Now's the time — you're not getting any older. Did you *meet someone?*

BUCK. Sort of.

DONNY. *Sort of?*

BUCK. I met this dog.

DONNY. That doesn't count, Buck —

BUCK. Couple weeks before the flood. Big, lovable mutt of a dog.

DONNY. I'm not asking about *animals.* I thought maybe you'd —

BUCK. I was in my yard, working on my stone fence.

DONNY. You're still at it with that fence?

BUCK. It never ends, Donny. I remove a few stones every day — but that thing is ENORMOUS. It'll take a *lifetime* to tear it down. But, anyway, I'm working on that fence and this stray dog wanders up and I'm petting it — and then I hear this whistle from across the road — this very loud and very clear whistle ... and the dog looks up ... and I look up ... and there, Donny ... standing there ... *(A long pause as the reverie stops Buck in his tracks. He stands, motionless on the ladder, a far away look on his face. Donny finally walks up close to the ladder and says, quietly —)*

DONNY. Buck?

BUCK. ... is this *woman.* And this is what I think to myself: I have seen the face of love. And at that moment, Donny, my life got very simple. I forgot all about the fence and the ark and saving mankind. I thought only of that face. *(Pause.)* And then she was gone. Walking into the distance with that dog at her side. And my reverie turned to panic — how will I find out who she is? How will I get in touch with her? *(Pause.)* So, I bought some meat.

DONNY. Some...?

BUCK. And every day I would set that meat out by the fence. And a *lot* of hungry animals came by — which was expensive, but saved me time later when I had to load the ark. Finally, yesterday, that dog came by. That lovable mutt of a dog. And I gave him some meat. And he gave me this — *(He produces a brightly colored dog's collar, with a large shiny tag attached.)* I know where she lives now, Donny. And I've got her number.

DONNY. You took the tag off her dog?!

BUCK. *(Sincerely.)* What would you have done?

DONNY. Well, I —

BUCK. And now that I've got her number and I've fallen in love with her, it feels only natural to give her a call — but according to you I should do the *opposite* of that.

DONNY. No, listen —

BUCK. But is the opposite of calling her NOT calling her? Or is it calling her and NOT saying what I want to say?

DONNY. Buck, wait —

BUCK. I'm new at this, Donny, and it's confusing. I don't even know her name, yet, but I think *she's the one.* I think she's the woman I want to grow young with. *(Donny stares at him.)*

DONNY. Call her up, Buck.

BUCK. Really?

DONNY. And tell her everything.

BUCK. I'm trusting you on this, Donny.

DONNY. If you're certain about it — do it now, while you can. Because, in time, the most certain things fade away.

BUCK. Like your work? *(Donny is silent.)* Why'd you give it up, Donny? *(Donny just smiles. Buck looks around.)* This used to be your office, didn't it?

DONNY. Yes.

BUCK. *(With relish, looking up at the skylight.)* It must have been a great escape. To come up here and gaze at the stars. Rita says you always used constellations — that your landscapes were always based on the formations of stars. Is that true?

DONNY. It's true.

BUCK. But why, Donny?

DONNY. There was a time when I wanted nothing more than to be transported to another world.

BUCK. I know the feeling. From the window of the ark I could see the whole world floating past. And for the first time, Donny, I knew my place in it. *(Donny looks at him, as — Buck turns and goes. A shaft of light isolates Louise in a separate, downstage area. She is dressed in her Act One clothes. She holds the blue sailor's cap in her hands. She speaks to the audience.)*

49

LOUISE. It's odd. When I look back, I remember it as the night I couldn't pray.

I left Donny standing there in his attic, and I drove home.

The house was dark.

I sat in my favorite chair.

I closed my eyes.

And I tried to pray.

But my mind kept racing — as though I were trying to sleep, the same relentless pounding in my head — and, try as I might, I couldn't quiet it.

I couldn't hear the sound of my own thoughts.

I turned on the lamp, looking for something to read.

And there beside me was Donny's portfolio.

I opened it.

And — one by one — I spread his designs and drawings all over the floor.

I sat for hours staring at them.

Alone in my house.

Surrounded by worlds.

When Rita called the next morning, I was still sitting there.

And I closed my eyes.

And I prayed. *(Lights shift back to the attic, where — Rita stands, neatly folding a man's shirt. We recognize this as Donny's Act One shirt. In front of her on the floor are two suitcases. One closed. One open. As Rita finishes folding the shirt — Donny enters and stands in the doorway, watching, as — Rita, kneels and packs the shirt carefully inside the open suitcase.)*

DONNY. Are you going somewhere?

RITA. *(Turns, smiles.)* You caught me.

DONNY. *(Curious.)* Well?

RITA. I'm not going anywhere, Donny. *We* are.

DONNY. Rita, what are you — *(Rita goes to a corner of the attic and retrieves an old picnic basket — the one we saw in Act One. She opens the lid and removes dozens of folded travel maps — placing them on the ground all around her, as she speaks —)*

RITA. I have maps, Donny. I have a LOT of maps. I've been collecting them since the day we got married. And I saved these maps so that one day — when we plan our honeymoon — we can

50

decide where we want to go —

DONNY. It's not time for our honeymoon, Rita. We've still got years together.

RITA. Maybe we should act like we don't.

DONNY. What are you saying — ?

RITA. A honeymoon is the last act of a marriage — one final adventure before we're swallowed up by youth. It's a *culmination*, Donny.

DONNY. Yes, I know that, but —

RITA. And maybe that's what we need. A "practice honeymoon." A trip to look at our lives before we get any younger.

DONNY. Rita —

RITA. A chance for you to start over. *(He stares at her as this phrase lands on him.)* Now, look at these and decide. I'll go anywhere you want — but we've got to go *somewhere*. We've got to get you out of this house.

DONNY. I know what you're doing, Rita —

RITA. Oh, do you? Then, help me out. Here's the itinerary. Tell me what you think. *(She hands a folded piece of paper to Donny. Donny says nothing.)* Okay. I thought we'd start with the arboretum you did — your first big job — laid out like the stars in Orion. Then we'll visit the gardens you did back East — the Corona Borealis. Then the park that won all the awards — based on Aquila — "The Eagle." And we'll end up at the project you abandoned, the design that was going to be your *crowning achievement*: the Steps to the Sea. They never hired another architect, you know. They're still waiting for you — just like I am. *(Donny folds the paper, hands it back to her and moves away.)*

    Donny, you sit in the cafe, day after day, staring out the window, scribbling away on napkins — *it's like you're drifting away, and I'm trying to make sense of it.* *(Donny says nothing.)* One year ago, you stopped working. And you never told me why. You said maybe, someday, you'd start again — but when? If you wait any longer, you'll be *too young* — you'll have too little time left. *(Moving to him, looking in his eyes.)* There's a *window*, Donny. A window of time for everything in our lives. And if we let that window close, that part of us is gone. *(Donny just stares at her.)* I wish you'd say something because I really want a cigarette and I'm too mad to kiss you.

DONNY. There's nothing to say, Rita.

RITA. *(Pause.)* Fine. We'll just —

DONNY. So, I'll say something: *(He stares at her, at a loss, then finally says —)*

DONNY. There's a movie we saw together, and in it —

RITA. Don't change the subj —

DONNY. I'm not — and in this movie, an astronaut is walking in space — all alone — tethered to the spacecraft by a single lifeline. And there's a mix-up of some kind. And his tether is released …

And he begins floating away … impossibly far away … into nothingness. *(Pause, he turns to her.)* When I worked, Rita, I would lose days. I would be transported to the landscape I was imagining. This was the secret of my success. And, at first, it was delicious — floating outside of my life, suspended in a world of my own devising. But, in time, Rita, *I could not get back.* Days and weeks would disappear as I made lines on the paper in front of me. But try as I might, I could not break its hold over me — *I could not get back to my life.*

RITA. I'd call that inspiration, Donny —

DONNY. It felt like death. And I didn't have the courage to face it. *(Pause.)* I wish I did. Sometimes I wish I could sever that cord and just *let go.*

RITA. *(Pause, with weight.)* Don't you dare. *(She looks at him for a long moment. Then, she approaches him and takes his face in her hands. Looks in his eyes.)* I didn't mind when you went away, Donny. Because I knew you'd reappear. It was your Last Great Trait — *you always reappeared. (He looks at her. She kisses him gently on the cheek, as — Trisha enters, quickly, saying —)*

TRISHA. Okay. Everything's worked out for the party. Angel's gonna come by later on — so we can still start at seven and then she'll — *(She stops.)* Did you really think you could surprise me? *(Donny and Rita nod.)* Very cute. *(As she goes.)* Nice banner. *(Trisha exits, as — Louise enters. She, too, is dressed differently than in Act One — with the most telling feature being her clerical collar.)*

LOUISE. I thought I was early. I thought the party wasn't until —

RITA. It's not.

LOUISE. She knows?

DONNY. She *thinks* she knows.

LOUISE. Very good. *(With gusto.)* Okay: Hi. Hi. How's things? Great. Now, first of all, I have a confession: I am wearing a phone. Now, I know you've got these silly rules at the Off-Line, but today I need you to make an exception.

RITA. Louise, you know you can't —

LOUISE. I mean it, Rita — I'm armed with a phone and *I am not to be messed with*. Because when you hear why — you'll be thrilled. Okay: Even though I head one of the smaller parishes in town, I pulled a few strings and got myself on the planning committee for the new seminary — you know, the one they're building out on the peninsula.

RITA. That's great.

LOUISE. That's not the news. This is the news: We met this morning to discuss the outdoor pavilion which will be the defining feature of the project. The committee considered a short list of architects (a very impressive list, I might add) — *(Shows them her phone.)* — and they made a recommendation which is being voted on *right now*. The vote is a formality, really. From what I can tell, the job is yours, Donny. Isn't that great?

RITA. Yes, it is. *(Silence.)* Donny —

DONNY. I gave that up, Louise — you know that.

LOUISE. But, this is the *perfect project*. A gathering place on a hillside — with paths leading down to the water. It's a smaller version of the one you abandoned.

DONNY. I didn't —

LOUISE. That's why I gave them your name. And after they saw your rough designs for Steps To The Sea, the room lit up — everyone agreed that you'd be —

DONNY. How did they get those designs?

LOUISE. I saved them. As many as I could grab the day you decided to purge your office.

DONNY. You had no right to show them those —

RITA. Donny, the least you can do is consider it —

DONNY. *(Forcefully, to Rita.)* How can you say that — after what I just told you?!

LOUISE. Are we supposed to feel bad for you? Is that it? That you can't design landscapes, anymore. That you've become a *busboy* at your wife's cafe?! Well, I'm sorry, Donny, but your application for *empathy* has been *denied*. I pulled strings — I lobbied *hard* to get on that committee —

DONNY. Well, you're wasting your time, all right?! I don't want your help. *(She steps toward him, speaks with a clear, sharp edge.)*

LOUISE. You lost your nerve. You had a crisis of faith. Well, how *hard* that must have been. And how remarkable that you were chosen — of all the people on this planet — that you were selected to have the *very first crisis of faith*. How must it feel to be so *special?!* *(Donny glares at Louise, but says nothing.)* Remember Donny: What you love about me is that I'm *direct*. *(Donny looks at her, then exits. Long silence, as the two women just stand in the room. Finally, Louise asks, quietly —)* Was I too harsh? I was afraid I'd lose my edge when I became a priest. Become sort of a mild-mannered pushover.

RITA. No danger of that, Louise. You still got it. *(Rita begins to put the maps back into the picnic basket. Louise helps her.)*

LOUISE. How've you done it, Rita?

RITA. Hmm?

LOUISE. Put up with him all these years.

RITA. I pretend I'm you. Whenever we hit a rough patch, I ask myself: What would Louise do in this situation?

LOUISE. *(With a laugh, curious.)* Why in the world would you do that?

RITA. *(Simply.)* I think you know. *(Pause.)* He still loves you. He always has. *(Pause.)* I know that circumstances never worked in your favor — which I'm grateful for, of course. But you must know it could have happened — that in a different world you and Donny would be together.

LOUISE. *(Pause; quietly.)* Yes.

RITA. I don't know how you do it. I don't know how you handle it with such grace.

LOUISE. *(Simply.)* I pray. *(Silence.)*

RITA. I can't do that.

LOUISE. Have you tried?

RITA. Yes.

LOUISE. And?

RITA. And I feel stupid.

LOUISE. Talking to the air?

RITA. Yes.

LOUISE. Asking for help from someone or something that may not even exist?

RITA. Yes — is that so strange?

LOUISE. What's strange is when you get an answer.

RITA. *(Pause, quietly.)* I never get an answer.

LOUISE. I'm sorry. *(Pause, quietly.)* Wish I could change that ... but I'm not on that committee. *(Rita looks at Louise, warmly.)*

RITA. What answer do you get? About Donny and his work?

LOUISE. It's not very uplifting, I'm afraid.

RITA. Try me.

LOUISE. That that which *drove us* — if left undone or incomplete — becomes that which *haunts us.* And unlike the things we never did, the things we *abandoned* haunt us forever. *(Donny enters and stands in the doorway.)*

DONNY. Louise? *(They both turn to him, expectantly.)*

LOUISE. Yes?

DONNY. Trisha's looking for you. *(Louise stares at Donny, looks back to Rita. Donny remains near the door.)*

RITA. I'll walk you down. *(The ringing of a cell phone is heard. Louise stares at Donny, as she removes it from her pocket, holds it out in front of her.)*

LOUISE. What'll it be, Donny?

DONNY. Withdraw my name. I mean it. *(She tosses him the ringing phone, saying —)*

LOUISE. Do it yourself. *(Louise goes. Rita stares at Donny, as — Donny looks down at the ringing phone, then back up at Rita, as — a shaft of light isolates Buck in a separate, downstage area. He wears his Act One clothing. He holds the Getz/Gilberto record album in his hands. He speaks to the audience.)*

BUCK. As I was pounding on the door, I heard music playing.

I guess Donny had run a wire from his stereo up into the attic. By the time I finally knocked the door down, the song had ended.

And, what's funny, is I keep thinking about the toast I made on his birthday. A bunch of us were out at a bar and I remembered a toast I'd heard overseas.

"Donny" — I said, lifting my glass — "I drink to your death. *(Pause.)* I will build your coffin myself from the wood of a one-hundred-year-old oak tree. *(Pause.)* I shall plant that tree tomorrow." *(Lights shift back to the attic, as — Donny enters, carrying several folding chairs in his arms. He is opening them and setting them in the room, as — Trisha enters. She carries a long, cardboard tube, sealed at the ends.)*

TRISHA. *(With a smile.)* Can I help?

DONNY. *(Pause, then relents.)* If you promise to act surprised.

TRISHA. It's a deal. *(She helps him set up the folding table in the room, and place the chairs around it, during the following. They also place a decorative tablecloth on the table.)* Why are we having the party up here?

DONNY. I'm sworn to secrecy. *(Referring to the tube.)* What's that?

TRISHA. Angel got me a poster for my birthday.

DONNY. Of what?

TRISHA. Space.

DONNY. I see.

TRISHA. *(Looking around the room.)* Hey, Dad.

DONNY. Hmm?

TRISHA. What ever happened to my recliner?

DONNY. Your what?

TRISHA. My reclining chair. The one I had when I was old. I thought you and Mom were going to store it up here for me.

DONNY. I'm afraid it's long gone, Trish.

TRISHA. But I loved that chair.

DONNY. I think we took it to the dump.

TRISHA. No way.

DONNY. Maybe we can get you another one. At a yard sale or something.

TRISHA. But, I *loved* that chair. I used to sit back and imagine all the things I was going to do when I got younger.

DONNY. And have you done them?

TRISHA. A few of them. Most were just dumb wishes. Things I knew I'd never do — but it was fun to pretend. *(Pause, she looks at him.)* Where do you think you'll go on your honeymoon?

DONNY. Oh, I don't know. Your mom's got a lot of maps.

TRISHA. Well, don't go where Shim and I went.

DONNY. I thought you drove up the coast —

TRISHA. — And visited every one of his relatives *one more time.*

56

Here it was, the last two weeks of our marriage — and we're play-ing charades with strange old Uncle Ed. It wasn't my idea of a honeymoon.

DONNY. Do you miss him?

TRISHA. Who? *(Smiles.)* You still can't say his name with a straight face.

DONNY. Sure I can.

TRISHA. Try it.

DONNY. Shim — there, okay? — I said it. Shim Shim Shim — see, no problem.

TRISHA. I miss him every day, without fail. *(Simply.)* But, we grow young ... and we say goodbye. *(Pause.)* Want to see my poster?

DONNY. Sure. *(Trisha removes the poster from the cardboard tube. She stands behind the table and prepares to open it.)*

TRISHA. Help me? *(Donny nods and holds one side of the poster. Trisha rolls the other side fully open onto the table. It is, in actuality, an architectural blueprint. Trisha looks down at it and smiles. Donny just stares at it.)* Pretty great, huh?

DONNY. Where'd you get this?

TRISHA. I told you.

DONNY. Did Louise give you this? *(No response.)* Trisha?

TRISHA. What's the big deal? You were going to throw it out, anyway — that's what Louise said.

DONNY. I don't care what she said, it doesn't —

TRISHA. I like it, okay?! And I'm keeping it. What's wrong with that? Why do you —

DONNY. It doesn't belong to you.

TRISHA. But, why can't I —

DONNY. *(Forcefully.)* Listen to me: Some things don't get shared, all right?! I'm sorry — but that's the way it is. Louise was not meant to have this. And neither are you. Do you understand? *(She stares at him, hurt. Finally ... she nods.)* Thank you.

TRISHA. *(Quietly.)* I'll get rid of it.

DONNY. Good.

TRISHA. I'll tear it up and throw it away.

DONNY. Fine.

TRISHA. It wouldn't have worked, anyway. Not as drawn. The steps are at the wrong angle coming down the cliffs. The afternoon light would be wasted. *(Donny looks at her. She steps away from the table.)* So, do me a favor. Tear it up for me. *(Silence. Donny looks down at the blueprint.)* What are you waiting for? It's not worth saving — you said so yourself. *(She approaches the table and reaches for the blueprint, saying —)* You want me to do it? *(His voice stops her. It is quiet and firm and focused — a man slowly, carefully trying to re-trace a road in his life.)*

DONNY. In the summer ... when the sun is high ... you're right — the angle is not ideal. But that's intentional — to let the light, instead, reflect from the sheer face of these rocks here — *(He shows her on the blueprint.)* and here ... keeping the main pathway partially shaded — and thus, more comfortable in the summer heat.

TRISHA. *(Pause.)* And in the winter? *(He looks at her. Then, he takes a long look at the blueprint. Speaks with quiet pride ...)*

DONNY. In the winter ... it's *perfect*. *(Donny slowly sits at the table, the blueprint in front of him. Trisha removes something from her pocket: a handful of paper napkins with drawings on them.)*

TRISHA. Circinus. *(SUR-seh-ness. Trisha sets the napkins — one by one — in front of Donny, atop the blueprint.)* You shouldn't leave your work lying around the cafe, Dad. The steps down the hill are laid out to match the seven stars which form Circinus — one of the smallest constellations in the southern hemisphere. Known as the Surveyor's Compass. *(Pause, refers to the napkins.)* It was your signature style: *the earth as a mirror to the heavens. (Donny takes one of the napkins from her. Looks at it.)* You haven't stopped working, have you? *(Donny is silent.)* That's why I chose you, you know. When I got young enough to go in search of parents. I liked the way you made worlds. *(Silence.)*

DONNY. *(Looking at the blueprint.)* But, to do this work, Trisha, I would have to leave. I would have to let go of my life.

TRISHA. Then, do it. Go where you've imagined. *(Their eyes meet.)* That's what I did. The best part of being an astronomer was thinking thoughts that were too big for my head. *(Trisha removes the covering from the telescope. She points the telescope in the direction of the skylight, looks through it, briefly.)* I was — at best — mediocre when it came to trajectories and mathematical probabilities of this-and-that-object in faraway space. But I was a hell of a dreamer. At night, in the observatory, my thoughts could travel without interruption.

58

I would imagine an astronaut saying goodbye to his wife and family.

I saw him strapped to a rocket.

And with a great roar of fire and smoke, he was launched to the far edge of the universe.

And when he arrived, he stepped out of the rocket.

And there in front of him was his house.

And in the doorway was his wife and family.

And though he had travelled a billion light-years away from home ... the world he found was the one he had left.

Identical in every way.

Or so it seemed.

DONNY. What was different?

TRISHA. People got *older*.

DONNY. What do you mean?

TRISHA. On this planet, time went backwards. And so, as the days went by, people did not grow young ... they grew old.

DONNY. That's impossible.

TRISHA. To our minds, yes. But we live in a tiny corner of space. Sheltered from such mysteries.

DONNY. But in a world like that, how would you know *how much life you had left?*

TRISHA. You wouldn't. There is *no countdown*. You reach a random number of years and it's over, you're gone.

DONNY. *(Pause.)* I can't imagine it.

TRISHA. It's weird, I know. *And:* you go on your honeymoon at the *beginning* of your marriage.

DONNY. When you hardly *know each other?*

TRISHA. And you do not choose your parents — you *inherit* them. And they watch as you get *bigger*, instead of smaller. And often, they die before you do.

DONNY. *(Pause, then he smiles.)* I can't twist my mind around that way —

TRISHA. It takes practice. But, even now, my working years behind me — I still think about those things. *(Wistfully.)* I still wonder what it would feel like to grow old. *(Silence ... as they think about this. Finally, Donny carefully rolls up the blueprint [and the napkins] and places it back in the tube. Trisha watches him.)*

Don't get mad at Louise — for giving me that.

DONNY. I won't. *(Trisha steps toward him, extends her hand.)*

TRISHA. Can I have it back?

DONNY. No. *(Donny looks at her, holding the tube.)* Remember: you promised to act surprised. *(Trisha stares at Donny, as — A shaft of light isolates Rita in a separate, downstage area. She wears her Act One clothing. She holds the photo album in her hands. She speaks to the audience.)*

RITA. I'm the one everyone asks.

It must have something to do with that whole Year of Being Real nonsense. They see me as the one person who will tell them the truth:

"What happened, Rita." "And why?"

That night, when I got home, I opened the suitcase Donny had filled for me. I went through my old books once again. And as I read, what had seemed, at the time, so complex and difficult to comprehend ... now seemed so simple.

I found a sentence I had underlined twenty years earlier.

And that one sentence gave me an answer to everyone's questions: "An act like this is prepared within the silence of the heart."

After Buck called the house, I ran into Trisha's room to tell her what had happened. But, she was gone. *(Lights shift back to the attic. It is night. Trisha, Louise and Buck are seated at the table. There are decorative drink cups on the table, as well as a covered dessert pan. Helium-filled birthday balloons frame the table. The cardboard tube holding the blueprint now sits on the shelf which held the cookies and record album in Act One. Downstage, away from the table, the two suitcases sit — closed, side by side.)*

TRISHA. So ... did you call her?

BUCK. *(Pause.)* I did. *(Trisha and Louise both hit him, excitedly.)* Ouch.

TRISHA and LOUISE. *And?*

BUCK. Now, don't push me. I'm not as experienced as you are.

LOUISE. What's her name?

BUCK. Her name ... is Grace.

TRISHA.   LOUISE.
Very nice.   Lovely.

BUCK. And she's a little ... *younger* than me. Is that bad?

60

TRISHA. Not at all.

LOUISE. That just means she's a little —

TRISHA. Smarter.

LOUISE. *(Correcting Trisha.) More worldly. (Buck produces the small notebook we saw in Act One, pages through it.)*

BUCK. I've been making a list of things to talk to her about. I'm so afraid I'll just freeze, just sit there with nothing to say —

LOUISE. You'll be fine.

TRISHA. I didn't have much in common with Shim when we first met, but I learned to —

LOUISE. Fake it.

TRISHA. *Adapt.* We learned each other's ways — and so will you.

LOUISE. Can we eat dessert now?! *(She reaches for the lid to the dessert plate, but Trisha slaps her hand away.)* What are we waiting for?!

TRISHA. *(To Buck.)* So, when will you see her?

BUCK. Sunday.

TRISHA. Excellent.

BUCK. We're going to hear Louise preach.

LOUISE. In Buck's honor, I'm speaking about the Flood.

TRISHA. You're going to *church*?! On your *first date*?!

BUCK. *(Genuine concern.)* Where should we go?

TRISHA. You should go off and be alone somewhere. Somewhere quiet —

LOUISE. It's quiet at church.

TRISHA. Some place with candlelight and —

LOUISE. We have candles.

TRISHA. And wine —

LOUISE. We —

TRISHA. *(To Louise.) Stop it. (To Buck.)* A place that will forever — from that day on — be *your place.*

BUCK. Where did you and Shim go?

TRISHA. *(A devilish smile.)* We came up here. *(Quickly.)* Don't tell Mom and Dad. *(Donny's voice is heard from off —)*

DONNY'S VOICE. COMING UP!

RITA'S VOICE. CLOSE YOUR EYES!

TRISHA. What are they —

BUCK.	LOUISE.
Close your eyes, Trisha —	Do as they say —

TRISHA. But, I —

BUCK and LOUISE. Ssshhh — *(Buck and Louise make sure Trisha's eyes are covered, as — Donny and Rita enter, carrying the recliner. It is covered not with the old tarp — but with a bright, festive piece of fabric of some kind. Wrapped around the recliner is a large, colorful ribbon and bow. Donny and Rita set it in its Act One position, as — Buck and Louise walk Trisha up close to it.)*

TRISHA. I don't trust any of you. Not a bit. What are you —

BUCK.	RITA.
Just another minute —	Almost ready —

DONNY. Okay. Three … Two … One …

EVERYONE. *(Except Trisha.)* SURPRISE! *(Trisha opens her eyes and sees the [covered] recliner. She is thrilled.)*

TRISHA. *(Quietly.)* Oh, I don't believe it. *(To Rita.)* Dad told me you'd taken it to the dump.

RITA. Believe me, I tried. *(Trisha smiles, as she removes the bow and the fabric, revealing the recliner — identical to Act One.)*

LOUISE. *(Shaking her head, baffled.)* Of all the things in the world you could ask for …

TRISHA. I know. It's *perfect* — isn't it? *(Looks, again, at Donny and Rita.)* May I?

DONNY. Please. *(Trisha sits, happily, in the recliner, as the others cheer/applaud.)*

RITA. Okay: Down to business.

LOUISE. Dessert! — finally!

DONNY. Not, yet.

RITA. Now: As you know, Trisha, there are certain traditions —

LOUISE. *(Correcting her.)* Rites of passage —

RITA. Whatever — associated with turning sixteen —

BUCK. The Three Great Rituals —

RITA. And that moment is now here. Are you ready?

TRISHA. Ready.

DONNY. Ritual Number One — *(Someone does a drum roll on a chair, as — Trisha proudly pulls a set of car keys — identical to Act One — from her pocket and holds them up.)*

RITA. — The Return of the Car Keys. *(Cheers/laughter as — Trisha hands the car keys to Donny.)*

TRISHA. Well, it was fun while it lasted.

LOUISE. No more traffic jams —

BUCK. *(Ribbing her.)* No more freedom —

TRISHA. Hey, don't laugh — your time will come.

RITA. Will you miss it?

TRISHA. Maybe. *(Leaning back in the recliner.)* But I'm looking forward to you and Dad *driving me everywhere.*

LOUISE. Moving along now — we've got dessert waiting —

RITA. Okay. Ritual Number Two — *(Another "drum roll," as — Donny produces a bottle of beer.)* — The Final Drink. *(Cheers/Laughter, as — Donny hands it, ceremonially, to Trisha.)*

TRISHA. Thank you.

RITA. We didn't know if you wanted beer or wine —

TRISHA. Beer is perfect.

BUCK. You know, Donny, I don't really like the taste of beer.

DONNY. Give it time — it'll grow on you.

TRISHA. *(Lifts the beer.)* Cheers!

DONNY, RITA, BUCK and LOUISE. *(Lifting their drinks.)* Cheers! *(They all drink. Rita hugs Trisha.)*

BUCK. *(To Donny, still re: beer.)* Plus, it always makes me so *sleepy.*

LOUISE. Oh, sure — rub it in.

RITA. *(To Louise.)* Still no luck, huh?

LOUISE. Oh, I miss how I used to sleep when I was older. The very first specialist I went to — years ago — asked me what place I most associated with being sleepy. I said "Church." He said "Try *that.*" Next thing you know I'm in the pulpit by day — and still *wide awake* at night. *(Buck lifts his glass, saying —)*

BUCK. To Louise and her sleep — *(The others lift their glasses, as well —)*

DONNY.	RITA.	TRISHA.
To her sleep —	Here, here —	To Louise —

(Now, they all begin to pull up chairs and/or gather on the floor near the recliner — near Trisha — as though gathering around an elder.)

TRISHA. *(Seeing them gather near her.)* Uh-oh, what now?

DONNY. Ritual Number Three —

TRISHA. And what's that?

RITA. — The Speech.

EVERYONE. *(Except Trisha.)* SPEECH! *(Etc. …)*

TRISHA. What do you want me to say?

63

BUCK. You're the sage of the house — give us wisdom!
TRISHA. Yeah, right.
LOUISE. *(A quick dig.)* Your dad, for one, could use some.
TRISHA. *(Turning to Rita.)* Mom, what should I —
RITA. Just tell us how it feels. None of us have been there. *(Trisha looks at the others. They wait.)*
TRISHA. Well ... thank you for the party. It was a *complete surprise.*
EVERYONE. *(Laughter.)* Yeah, right. / Sure it was. / *(Etc ...)*
TRISHA. And thanks for putting up with me all these years.
RITA.

RITA.	BUCK.	LOUISE.
It's been a joy.	Our pleasure.	It was hell.

(Laughter/smiles. Then ... silence. Trisha looks at each of them once again — and, in doing so, seems to find the words ...)
TRISHA. Well ... *(Pause.)* I've had a rich and full life ... and now I am ready to enter my childhood. I look forward to the mystery of my final years — when the world grows new and simple once again ... and I am given the clarity of innocence. There are things I never did. And I regret them. There are people I hurt. And I beg their forgiveness. And there are doors I never opened which will haunt me to my final years. But, in that brief window of days when life was still mine to shape, I did what I could to leave some trace of my time on earth. And now, as I grow small and weak, I ask for your prayers.

Remember me fondly. Speak of me often. And *travel further, dig deeper,* and *risk more* than I ever did.

For the future's one reward is a memorable past.

Keep faith.

And sing your life.

No matter what else ... *take it* ... and *sing it.* *(She finishes her speech looking directly at Donny. He looks at her, moved ... and nods. Silence for a long moment ... then Donny says, quietly ...)*
DONNY. Happy Birthday, Trisha.
RITA, LOUISE and BUCK. Happy Birthday. *(Trisha embraces Donny, as — Rita moves to the covered dessert plate, saying —)*
RITA. And now, by special request of Louise — and in honor of the Birthday Girl — I would like to present: *(Rita uncovers the plate, revealing —)*

TRISHA. PIE!

LOUISE. I'm in heaven. *(As the others converge on the table and surround the pie — Donny has gone to the attic door and is looking downstairs. Rita is about to cut the pie, when —)*

DONNY. Rita, wait. *(Rita stops. Louise — leaning over the pie — shoots Donny a look —)*

LOUISE. This better be good.

DONNY. They're here.

RITA. Already? What time is it?

TRISHA. Who's here?

BUCK. Yeah, who's here?

TRISHA. Mom, what's —

RITA. The fact is, Trisha — this isn't the party. *(Smiles.)* The real party is downstairs.

DONNY, RITA and LOUISE. Surprise!

TRISHA. But, Angel told me none of my friends could —

RITA. It was all part of the plan.

LOUISE. We're just the warm-up act.

TRISHA. You lured me up here, while they were —

RITA. C'mon — everyone's waiting.

TRISHA. I don't believe this.

LOUISE. I'm bringing the pie.

RITA. Don't worry — there's more downstairs. And grab the chairs — we'll need them. *(Louise and Rita exit, carrying away the table, as Donny folds up the chairs, etc. Trisha and Buck sit/stand staring at each other.)*

BUCK. I had no part in this, Trisha. Ever since the Flood nobody tells me anything.

TRISHA. You and me have to stick together, Buck. *(They start out, taking the balloons with them.)*

BUCK. Donny, c'mon —

DONNY. I'll be right there. *(Buck and Trisha exit, leaving Donny alone in the now quiet, empty room. Donny pulls the bundled of extension cord from the outlet, as the lights go out. Moonlight illuminates the recliner. A huge cheer of "SURPRISE" is heard from off — from downstairs. Donny is about to leave the room, then stops. He goes the shelf and takes down the cardboard tube. He removes the blueprint and holds it in his hands. His eyes fall on the two suitcases. Carrying the blueprint, he goes to the suitcases, and kneels near them. After a moment, Rita appears in the doorway behind Donny. He does not see her. Donny sets the blueprint down and opens "his" suitcase, looks inside. He removes something: it is a small leather pouch which holds his drafting pencils.)*

RITA. *(Quietly, hopefully.)* Did you change your mind? *(Donny looks back at her, but says nothing.)* We're packed and ready to go. One suitcase each. And Buck's agreed to cover the cafe while were gone. *(Still nothing from Donny.)* I even packed your drafting pencils. Just in case. *(Rita steps into the room, kneels near him.)* It will be a great adventure, Donny. And when we get back, we'll go to work on this room — we'll get your studio set up again. *(Donny lifts a photo album — identical to Act One — from out of his suitcase. The music from downstairs has faded out.)*

DONNY. What's this?

RITA. *(Smiles.)* Just some old pictures. Thought our trip might be a good time to reminisce. *(Donny opens the album and looks at the pictures. Rita moves in close to him, also looking.)* God, who were those people? *(They turn pages in the album.)* Hey, Donny?

DONNY. Hmm?

RITA. Do you wish I was still old? *(She refers to the album, wistfully.)* Look at me — how white my hair was.

DONNY. It was gorgeous.

RITA . And my face ... *(Still looking, as she touches her own face.)* All my best lines are gone now. *(Donny gently touches her face.)*

DONNY. You're still lovely, Rita.

RITA. Even now that I'm young? *(Donny nods. Silence. She looks at him.)* What made you change your mind?

DONNY. *(Quietly.)* You did. All of you did.

RITA. *(With a smile.)* We should tell Louise the answer is "Yes" — that you'll accept the project.

DONNY. They never offered it. *(Pause.)* When I spoke to them they said they'd had a change of heart. They decided to go with someone older, someone with a fresh outlook. *(Pause.)* Someone who could finish what he started.

RITA. *(Pause.)* I'm sorry.

DONNY. You were right, Rita. It's time to start over. *(Pause.)* It's time to go on our honeymoon. *(She looks at him. He returns her look.)*

RITA. A practice one, you mean.

DONNY. No. *(Pause.)* A true one. A culmination. *(Silence.)*

RITA. *(Quietly.)* And then?

DONNY. And then I'll do as you asked. I'll return to my work.

RITA. Alone? *(Silence, as Rita stares at him.)* That's not what I asked, Donny. I didn't ask you to leave.

DONNY. I won't stay in this house like a ghost, Rita. I won't do that to you and Trisha.

RITA. So, you'll — what? — you'll abandon us like you did your work? You really think that's the answer?!

DONNY. You want it made simple, Rita, but it —

RITA. No, I don't. I want it made *difficult*. I want it to be *impossible* for you to leave.

DONNY. Rita —

RITA. *I'm not ready to say goodbye to you.* Don't you see that?! I don't have the words. *(Pause.)* Do you? *(Long silence. Finally ... more quietly.)* I always feared it would be me. That would want out. If it happened — and I prayed it would not — I always feared it would be me. *(Silence. Then, flatly ...)* Well. It's a great night for a party. *(She turns to Donny.)* Don't tell, Trisha. Not tonight.

DONNY. I won't. *(Pause, quietly.)* Will you walk down with me? *(During the following, Rita picks up the photo album and holds it.)*

RITA. *(Simply.)* No.

DONNY. What should I tell them?

RITA. Tell them I'm having a cigarette. *(Donny stares at her, approaches her —)*

DONNY. Rita —

RITA. *(Sharp.)* What is it you *want*? You want my *blessing*?! Well, I can't give you that. I plan to be very mad at you for a very long time.

DONNY. What I want, Rita, is to make this trip — the trip you planned for us. And maybe, as we travel, we'll find the words.

RITA. Don't make it sound simple. You've made your decision — and it feels clean to you. Decisions always feel clean to the person who's leaving. *(Quiet, sharp.)* But for those of us left behind ... it's *messy*, Donny. It's messy — and it is *not simple*. *(Donny looks at Rita, then goes. When he is gone, Rita sits in the recliner, holding the photo album tightly, staring up at the skylight, as — a shaft of light isolates Trisha in a separate, downstage area. She wears her Act One*

clothing. She holds the car keys in her hand. She speaks to the audience.)
TRISHA. I got in the car and started it up.
   I couldn't believe I was actually driving Dad's convertible.
   Buck followed me home, and as I turned onto our street —
he honked and waved and drove away.
   I saw the light on in Mom's room.
   I started to pull into our driveway ... but didn't.
   Within minutes I was on the highway.
   And soon after that I took an exit and found myself in the
country.
   A winding road I remembered from when I was little.
   The city lights like a memory in the distance.
   And as I drove, I pushed the button on the dash ... and the
convertible top lifted and came down ... revealing the stars.
   The wind whipped my hair against my face.
   The moon glowed in the rear-view.
   And I drove for hours.
   In the middle of nowhere, in the middle of the night ...
thinking about my dad.
   And I felt something for the first time.
   For the first time in my life, I felt completely free.
   And I wondered if he did. *(Sound of a steady rain, as — lights
shift back to the attic. It is nearly identical to the end of Act One: The
recliner sits in its position, uncovered. The Signal Box sits next to it —
but now its casing has been torn open, revealing the wires inside. The
Getz/Gilberto record album leans against the jar of cookies on the
shelf, upstage. The vintage transit on the tripod is where we left it. The
bundle of cords is plugged in, the lamps are lit. In addition: The door
— still off its hinges — remains leaning against a wall, where it was
in Act Two. As Trisha turns and steps into the room — Buck, in his
Act One clothing, comes up the stairs, carrying a few large cardboard
boxes. Hanging from his wrist is the black umbrella, unopened, but
wet. They look at each other, but do not speak. Buck sets the boxes in
the room, and shakes the umbrella dry, as — Louise — in her Act One
clothing — comes up the stairs. She also carries a few cardboard boxes
of varying sizes. She sets the boxes in the room — a few feet away from
those Buck placed. From one of the boxes, she removes the blue sailor's
cap — and holds it. She turns to Trisha.)*

68

LOUISE. *(Quietly.)* Is your mom coming?

TRISHA. Yes. *(Louise goes to Trisha and embraces her.)*

LOUISE. This was a good idea, Trisha.

TRISHA. The house felt so empty. I thought we should bring a few of his things back up here.

LOUISE. I have something else in my car. I'll be right back. *(Louise starts out — hanging the sailor's cap on the transit tripod, as she goes. Buck removes the saw Donny gave him from one of the boxes, and hangs it on a wall. Then, he begins looking at the pried-open Signal Box.)*

TRISHA. Was it an accident? *(Buck turns to her, says nothing.)* Tell me the truth.

BUCK. I don't know.

TRISHA. You said he might have spliced the wrong wire. He may have activated the gas by mistake. *(Buck looks at her.)* Were you just *saying that?*

BUCK. Trisha —

TRISHA. He could have made a mistake. He might not have known.

BUCK. You're right.

TRISHA. And, he had the tarp against the bottom of the door to make the room *dark* — that's what he told me — *completely dark.* Not because he wanted to —

BUCK. Ssshhh —

TRISHA. I want to talk about this! When you knocked the door down, what did you see?

BUCK. Trisha —

TRISHA. Was he in the chair?

BUCK. No, he wasn't.

TRISHA. *(Adamantly.)* See — it was an *accident.* He was choking on the gas and he was trying to get out. That's why the skylight was broken. He wanted to —

BUCK. The firemen broke the glass — to air out the room —

TRISHA. But they said it was cracked. That maybe he — *(Buck looks in her eyes, holding her.)*

BUCK. No one knows, Trish. We have to accept that. No one will *ever know.* *(Rita, also in her Act One clothing, enters. She stands in the doorway for a moment, holding a folded newspaper. She looks at*

69

the room.)
RITA. *(Quietly.)* It feels so small. Why does a room with nothing in it feel so small?
BUCK. *(Going to Rita.)* How you holding up?
RITA. I'll never forgive him. He never gave me a chance to say goodbye. *(Pause, to Buck.)* Are you the reason for all this rain?
BUCK. Who told you about that? *(Rita puts her arms around Buck.)* No. The voices have stopped. Whatever they were —. they're gone. My house is just like this now ... quiet. Very quiet. *(Louise enters, carrying Donny's portfolio. She sets it in a prominent place in the room.)*
LOUISE. Is that your briefcase downstairs, Rita?
RITA. Yes.
LOUISE. It's ringing. Or beeping. Or something.
RITA. *(Not moving.)* Thanks.
LOUISE. Do you need to —
RITA. *(Quietly.)* No. Not today. *(Louise goes to the recliner and sits — looking up in the direction of the skylight.)*
BUCK. What will happen to the house?
RITA. I was just telling Louise — he paid it off. All of it. And he never told me. He put it in my name — so I could sell it when I wanted to.
BUCK. Are you going to?
RITA. No. I think I'll hold onto it. I'm determined to have the last word. *(They are all silent for a moment.)*
LOUISE. *(Softly, looking out the skylight.)* "Thy steadfast love, Oh Lord, extends to the heavens; thy faithfulness to the clouds." *(More silence. Then, Rita hands Trisha the newspaper.)*
TRISHA. Is it in here?
RITA. *(Nods, to Buck and Louise.)* Trisha wanted to write it herself.
LOUISE. Let's hear it.
TRISHA. Mom? *(Rita nods, as Buck puts his arms around her. Trisha looks at them, then reads from the paper.)* "Donny Edward Rowan. Age forty-three. Devoted father and friend. He will be remembered in our hearts forever. And he will be missed not only for who he was, but for who he might have become. We hope and pray that he has found peace. And we know that wherever he is, he is taking the measure of the sky." *(Silence.)*

70

LOUISE. It's lovely.

RITA. Yes. *(Silence, as — Louise settles back into the reclining chair. Buck stares up at the skylight. Rita slowly looks around the room.)*

TRISHA. *(Going to Rita.)* Buck's invited us over for dinner.

RITA. *(Pause, then nods.)* We'll need to take your car.

TRISHA. Okay. *(To Buck.)* Should we bring anything? *(No response, as Buck continues to look up at the skylight.)* Buck?

BUCK. *(Quietly, simply.)* I should have gone with him. We're meant to travel in pairs. Two by two. *(Buck looks around the room and then says, softly —)* Goodbye, friend. *(Music plays. Donny enters, wearing his Act One clothes. He carries the suitcase from Act Two in his hand. He stops at the doorway and looks into the room. Donny is not seen by the others, nor does he see them.)*

TRISHA. *(Going to Buck.)* We'll bring dessert. How's that?

BUCK. Sounds great. *(Donny sets the suitcase down. He lifts the door from its position against the wall. He carries it into the room and lays it across the two stacks of boxes which Buck and Louise just brought in ... forming a makeshift desk, with the suitcase as his chair. As he does this — Rita is looking at the Getz/Gilberto record album.)*

TRISHA. What's that, Mom?

RITA. Just history. *(She puts the album back in its place, turns to Trisha.)* We should go. Before the rain gets any worse. *(Donny sets a small lamp from the room atop the desk. He removes his drafting pencils from the suitcase.)* Why don't you go down and start the car? *(Trisha nods and goes to the door. Buck follows her, carrying the umbrella. He says to Rita —)*

BUCK. We'll see you there. *(Rita nods. As Buck and Trisha are leaving, they see that Louise has fallen asleep in the chair.)*

TRISHA. What about Louise? Should we —

BUCK. *(Quietly.)* No. She's fine. Let her sleep. *(Music continues and builds, as — Buck puts his arm around Trisha, and they leave. Rita looks back at the record album, changing her mind. Donny goes to his portfolio and removes a sheet of drafting paper from it. On the way back to his desk, he sees the jar of cookies. Donny lifts the jar of cookies at the same moment that Rita lifts the record album. Rita moves to the doorway, carrying the album, as — Donny sets the jar of cookies, and the drafting paper, on his desk. He sits. Rita takes one last look at the room, holding the album tightly against her chest. Rita*

71

unplugs the extension cords at the same moment that Donny turns his desk lamp "on" — the lamp "lights" as the room goes dark — except for a shaft of moonlight on Louise in the chair. Rita turns and leaves, as — the music plays and the rain continues. Louise sleeps in the chair. Donny starts to open the jar of cookies, then stops, remembering something. He reaches into his shirt pocket and removes the cookie he placed there at the end of Act One. He takes a bite of the cookie, and then — He begins to do his work. He sketches with the pencil, as — the music concludes, and the — Lights fade to black.)

End of Play

PROPERTY LIST

Surveying transit on tripod, covered with blanket
Party things: balloons, covered cake pan, drink cups
Cardboard boxes (DONNY, BUCK)
Extension cords and adapters (DONNY)
Crosswalk signal box (DONNY, TRISHA)
Large handsaw (BUCK)
Wallet and bills (BUCK)
Pocket watch (BUCK)
Mail (BUCK)
Astronomy magazines (BUCK)
Toys (TRISHA)
Glass jar filled with cookies (TRISHA, DONNY)
Red wagon (DONNY)
Record Album (DONNY, RITA)
Rag (DONNY)
Briefcase (RITA)
Cell phone (RITA, LOUISE)
Photo album (RITA, DONNY)
Vintage suitcase (DONNY)
Book: *The Myth of Sisyphus* (DONNY)
Blue sailor's cap (LOUISE, BUCK)
Picnic basket (DONNY, RITA)
Small notebook (BUCK)
Old black umbrella (BUCK, RITA)
Large, old leather portfolio (LOUISE)
Recliner (covered by tarp) (DONNY)
Key ring with 2 keys (DONNY, TRISHA)
Orange life-preserver (BUCK)
Folding table (DONNY, RITA, LOUISE)
Door (DONNY)
Wooden ladder (RITA, BUCK, DONNY)
2 vintage suitcases (DONNY, RITA)
Telescope on tripod, covered with tarp (RITA)
Olive branch with a few leaves (BUCK)
Cook's apron (RITA, DONNY)
Birthday banner (DONNY, RITA)

Man's shirt (RITA)
Dog collar with tags (BUCK)
Travel maps (RITA)
Folded piece of paper (RITA)
Folding chairs (DONNY)
Tablecloth (DONNY)
Long cardboard tube (TRISHA, DONNY)
Blueprint (TRISHA, DONNY)
Paper napkins with drawings (TRISHA, DONNY)
Bottle of beer (DONNY)
Pie and pie cutter (RITA)
Leather pouch with drafting pencils (DONNY)
Newspaper (RITA)
Drafting paper (DONNY)

SOUND EFFECTS

Cell phone ring
Buck's voice on tape
Crash of door being kicked in
Rain

NEW PLAYS

★ **THE EXONERATED by Jessica Blank and Erik Jensen.** Six interwoven stories paint a picture of an American criminal justice system gone horribly wrong and six brave souls who persevered to survive it. "The #1 play of the year...intense and deeply affecting..." –*NY Times*. "Riveting. Simple, honest storytelling that demands reflection." –*A.P.* "Artful and moving...pays tribute to the resilience of human hearts and minds." –*Variety*. "Stark...riveting...cunningly orchestrated." –*The New Yorker*. "Hard-hitting, powerful, and socially relevant." –*Hollywood Reporter*. [7M, 3W] ISBN: 0-8222-1946-8

★ **STRING FEVER by Jacquelyn Reingold.** Lily juggles the big issues: turning forty, artificial insemination and the elusive scientific Theory of Everything in this Off-Broadway comedy hit. "Applies the elusive rules of string theory to the conundrums of one woman's love life. Think *Sex and the City* meets *Copenhagen*." –*NY Times*. "A funny offbeat and touching look at relationships...an appealing romantic comedy populated by oddball characters." –*NY Daily News*. "Where kooky, zany, and madcap meet...whimsically winsome." –*NY Magazine*. "STRING FEVER will have audience members happily stringing along." –*TheaterMania.com*. "Reingold's language is surprising, inventive, and unique." –*nytheatre.com*. "...[a] whimsical comic voice." –*Time Out*. [3M, 3W (doubling)] ISBN: 0-8222-1952-2

★ **DEBBIE DOES DALLAS adapted by Erica Schmidt, composed by Andrew Sherman, conceived by Susan L. Schwartz.** A modern morality tale told as a comic musical of tragic proportions as the classic film is brought to the stage. "A scream! A saucy, tongue-in-cheek romp." –*The New Yorker*. "Hilarious! DEBBIE manages to have it all: beauty, brains and a great sense of humor!" –*Time Out*. "Shamelessly silly, shrewdly self-aware and proud of being naughty. Great fun!" –*NY Times*. "Racy and raucous, a lighthearted, fast-paced thoroughly engaging and hilarious send-up." –*NY Daily News*. [3M, 5W] ISBN: 0-8222-1955-7

★ **THE MYSTERY PLAYS by Roberto Aguirre-Sacasa.** Two interrelated one acts, loosely based on the tradition of the medieval mystery plays. "... stylish, spine-tingling...Mr. Aguirre-Sacasa uses standard tricks of horror stories, borrowing liberally from masters like Kafka, Lovecraft, Hitchcock...But his mastery of the genre is his own...irresistible." –*NY Times*. "Undaunted by the special-effects limitations of theatre, playwright and *Marvel* comic-book writer Roberto Aguirre-Sacasa maps out some creepy twilight zones in THE MYSTERY PLAYS, an engaging, related pair of one acts...The theatre may rarely deliver shocks equivalent to, say, *Dawn of the Dead*, but Aguirre-Sacasa's work is fine compensation." –*Time Out*. [4M, 2W] ISBN: 0-8222-2038-5

★ **THE JOURNALS OF MIHAIL SEBASTIAN by David Auburn.** This epic one-man play spans eight tumultuous years and opens a uniquely personal window on the Romanian Holocaust and the Second World War. "Powerful." –*NY Times*. "[THE JOURNALS OF MIHAIL SEBASTIAN] allows us to glimpse the idiosyncratic effects of that awful history on one intelligent, pragmatic, recognizably real man..." –*NY Newsday*. [3M, 5W] ISBN: 0-8222-2006-7

★ **LIVING OUT by Lisa Loomer.** The story of the complicated relationship between a Salvadoran nanny and the Anglo lawyer she works for. "A stellar new play. Searingly funny." –*The New Yorker*. "Both generous and merciless, equally enjoyable and disturbing." –*NY Newsday*. "A bitingly funny new comedy. The plight of working mothers is explored from two pointedly contrasting perspectives in this sympathetic, sensitive new play." –*Variety*. [2M, 6W] ISBN: 0-8222-1994-8

DRAMATISTS PLAY SERVICE, INC.
440 Park Avenue South, New York, NY 10016   212-683-8960   Fax 212-213-1539
postmaster@dramatists.com   www.dramatists.com

NEW PLAYS

★ **MATCH by Stephen Belber.** Mike and Lisa Davis interview a dancer and choreographer about his life, but it is soon evident that their agenda will either ruin or inspire them— and definitely change their lives forever. "Prolific laughs and ear-to-ear smiles." *–NY Magazine.* "Uproariously funny, deeply moving, enthralling theater. Stephen Belber's MATCH has great beauty and tenderness, and abounds in wit." *–NY Daily News.* "Three and a half out of four stars." *–USA Today.* "A theatrical steeplechase that leads straight from outrageous bitchery to unadorned, heartfelt emotion." *–Wall Street Journal.* [2M, 1W] ISBN: 0-8222-2020-2

★ **HANK WILLIAMS: LOST HIGHWAY by Randal Myler and Mark Harelik.** The story of the beloved and volatile country-music legend Hank Williams, featuring twenty-five of his most unforgettable songs. "[LOST HIGHWAY has] the exhilarating feeling of Williams on stage in a particular place on a particular night...serves up classic country with the edges raw and the energy hot...By the end of the play, you've traveled on a profound emotional journey: LOST HIGHWAY transports its audience and communicates the inspiring message of the beauty and richness of Williams' songs...forceful, clear-eyed, moving, impressive." *–Rolling Stone.* "...honors a very particular musical talent with care and energy... smart, sweet, poignant." *–NY Times.* [7M, 3W] ISBN: 0-8222-1985-9

★ **THE STORY by Tracey Scott Wilson.** An ambitious black newspaper reporter goes against her editor to investigate a murder and finds the *best* story...but at what cost? "A singular new voice...deeply emotional, deeply intellectual, and deeply musical..." *–The New Yorker.* "...a conscientious and absorbing new drama..." *–NY Times.* "...a riveting, tough-minded drama about race, reporting and the truth..." *–A.P.* "... a stylish, attention-holding script that ends on a chilling note that will leave viewers with much to talk about." *–Curtain Up.* [2M, 7W (doubling, flexible casting)] ISBN: 0-8222-1998-0

★ **OUR LADY OF 121st STREET by Stephen Adly Guirgis.** The body of Sister Rose, beloved Harlem nun, has been stolen, reuniting a group of life-challenged childhood friends who square off as they wait for her return. "A scorching and dark new comedy... Mr. Guirgis has one of the finest imaginations for dialogue to come along in years." *–NY Times.* "Stephen Guirgis may be the best playwright in America under forty." *–NY Magazine.* [8M, 4W] ISBN: 0-8222-1965-4

★ **HOLLYWOOD ARMS by Carrie Hamilton and Carol Burnett.** The coming-of-age story of a dreamer who manages to escape her bleak life and follow her romantic ambitions to stardom. Based on Carol Burnett's bestselling autobiography, *One More Time.* "...pure theatre and pure entertainment..." *–Talkin' Broadway.* "...a warm, fuzzy evening of theatre." *–BrodwayBeat.com.* "...chuckles and smiles of recognition or surprise flow naturally...a remarkable slice of life." *–TheatreScene.net.* [5M, 5W, 1 girl] ISBN: 0-8222-1959-X

★ **INVENTING VAN GOGH by Steven Dietz.** A haunting and hallucinatory drama about the making of art, the obsession to create and the fine line that separates truth from myth. "Like a van Gogh painting, Dietz's story is a gorgeous example of excess—one that remakes reality with broad, well-chosen brush strokes. At evening's end, we're left with the author's resounding opinions on art and artifice, and provoked by his constant query into which is greater: van Gogh's art or his violent myth." *–Phoenix New Times.* "Dietz's writing is never simple. It is always brilliant. Shaded, compressed, direct, lucid—he frames his subject with a remarkable understanding of painting as a physical experience." *–Tucson Citizen.* [4M, 1W] ISBN: 0-8222-1954-9

DRAMATISTS PLAY SERVICE, INC.
440 Park Avenue South, New York, NY 10016 212-683-8960 Fax 212-213-1539
postmaster@dramatists.com www.dramatists.com

NEW PLAYS

★ **INTIMATE APPAREL by Lynn Nottage.** The moving and lyrical story of a turn-of-the-century black seamstress whose gifted hands and sewing machine are the tools she uses to fashion her dreams from the whole cloth of her life's experiences. "…Nottage's play has a delicacy and eloquence that seem absolutely right for the time she is depicting…" –*NY Daily News.* "…thoughtful, affecting…The play offers poignant commentary on an era when the cut and color of one's dress—and of course, skin—determined whom one could and could not marry, sleep with, even talk to in public." –*Variety.* [2M, 4W] ISBN: 0-8222-2009-1

★ **BROOKLYN BOY by Donald Margulies.** A witty and insightful look at what happens to a writer when his novel hits the bestseller list. "The characters are beautifully drawn, the dialogue sparkles…" –*nytheatre.com.* "Few playwrights have the mastery to smartly investigate so much through a laugh-out-loud comedy that combines the vintage subject matter of successful writer-returning-to-ethnic-roots with the familiar mid-life crisis." –*Show Business Weekly.* [4M, 3W] ISBN: 0-8222-2074-1

★ **CROWNS by Regina Taylor.** Hats become a springboard for an exploration of black history and identity in this celebratory musical play. "Taylor pulls off a Hat Trick: She scores thrice, turning CROWNS into an artful amalgamation of oral history, fashion show, and musical theater…" –*TheatreMania.com.* "…wholly theatrical…Ms. Taylor has created a show that seems to arise out of spontaneous combustion, as if a bevy of department-store customers simultaneously decided to stage a revival meeting in the changing room." –*NY Times.* [1M, 6W (2 musicians)] ISBN: 0-8222-1963-8

★ **EXITS AND ENTRANCES by Athol Fugard.** The story of a relationship between a young playwright on the threshold of his career and an aging actor who has reached the end of his. "[Fugard] can say more with a single line than most playwrights convey in an entire script…Paraphrasing the title, it's safe to say this drama, making its memorable entrance into our consciousness, is unlikely to exit as long as a theater exists for exceptional work." –*Variety.* "A thought-provoking, elegant and engrossing new play…" –*Hollywood Reporter.* [2M] ISBN: 0-8222-2041-5

★ **BUG by Tracy Letts.** A thriller featuring a pair of star-crossed lovers in an Oklahoma City motel facing a bug invasion, paranoia, conspiracy theories and twisted psychological motives. "…obscenely exciting…top-flight craftsmanship. Buckle up and brace yourself…" –*NY Times.* "…[a] thoroughly outrageous and thoroughly entertaining play…the possibility of enemies, real and imagined, to squash has never been more theatrical." –*A.P.* [3M, 2W] ISBN: 0-8222-2016-4

★ **THOM PAIN (BASED ON NOTHING) by Will Eno.** An ordinary man muses on childhood, yearning, disappointment and loss, as he draws the audience into his last-ditch plea for empathy and enlightenment. "It's one of those treasured nights in the theater—treasured nights anywhere, for that matter—that can leave you both breathless with exhilaration and…in a puddle of tears." –*NY Times.* "Eno's words…are familiar, but proffered in a way that is constantly contradictory to our expectations. Beckett is certainly among his literary ancestors." –*nytheatre.com.* [1M] ISBN: 0-8222-2076-8

★ **THE LONG CHRISTMAS RIDE HOME by Paula Vogel.** Past, present and future collide on a snowy Christmas Eve for a troubled family of five. "…[a] lovely and hauntingly original family drama…a work that breathes so much life into the theater." –*Time Out.* "…[a] delicate visual feast…" –*NY Times.* "…brutal and lovely…the overall effect is magical." –*NY Newsday.* [3M, 3W] ISBN: 0-8222-2003-2

DRAMATISTS PLAY SERVICE, INC.
440 Park Avenue South, New York, NY 10016 212-683-8960 Fax 212-213-1539
postmaster@dramatists.com www.dramatists.com